Late Capitalist Freud in Literary, Cultural, and Political Theory

Maria-Daniella Dick • Robbie McLaughlan

Late Capitalist Freud in Literary, Cultural, and Political Theory

palgrave
macmillan

Maria-Daniella Dick
School of Critical Studies
University of Glasgow
Glasgow, UK

Robbie McLaughlan
School of English Literature
Language and Linguistics
Newcastle University
Newcastle, UK

ISBN 978-3-030-47193-4 ISBN 978-3-030-47194-1 (eBook)
https://doi.org/10.1007/978-3-030-47194-1

This Palgrave Macmillan imprint is published by the registered company Springer Nature Switzerland AG.
The registered company address is: Gewerbestrasse 11, 6330 Cham, Switzerland

To Vassiliki Kolocotroni

Acknowledgments

Our thanks to the departments of English Literature at the University of Glasgow and Newcastle University, which have supported us and granted research leave to work on this book.

We would like to thank friends in both Newcastle and Glasgow: John Coyle, Taylor Driggers, Faye Hammill, Katherine Heavey, Donald Mackenzie, Andrew Radford, Bryony Randall, Matt Sangster, Richard Stacey, Helen Stoddart, Zoë Strachan, Adrian Streete, Louise Welsh and Anne Whitehead.

A special thanks to James Annesley, who has supported this project from its inception and offered friendship and guidance beyond it. Thanks also to James Procter for his faith that we would reach the end.

We thank friends, colleagues and comrades elsewhere: Martin Dubois, Adam Kelly, Sadek Kessous, Graeme MacDonald, Eliza O'Brien, Stephen Shapiro, David Stewart and Alex Thomson.

Our solidarity to the students of Modernities MLitt past and present (of whom we are two).

We are grateful for all that we share together with Sophie Vlacos and Ciarán Jenkins, Rhian Williams and Alex Benchimol, Neelam Srivastava, Martin Izod and Jess Corbett, Laura Miller and Luke McAllister, and Meiko O'Halloran and Jon Quayle.

To our parents Fiona and William Dick, Gerry and Kate McLaughlan for all that they continue to give us and more; and to Jamie and Elianna, John and Saskia and all our family.

For the wee ones that we love, who we hope will grow up in a world after capitalism: Ella (5 months), Ada (6 months), Alessia (1), Dominic (2), Mary (3) and Nia (5). You have a world to win.

We thank the staff at the Mitchell Library in Glasgow, who provided a space to write.

At Palgrave Macmillan, we offer grateful thanks to Allie Troyanos and to Rachel Jacobe and Vinoth Kuppan.

We would like finally to mark our gratitude to Arthur Kroker and the late Marilouise Kroker, who offered support and legitimacy to this project in its early stages by accepting a version of Chap. 3 for publication in *CTheory.net*, whose faith seeded confidence in its ideas and ultimately allowed us the special experience of working together on this book. We are grateful to *CTheory.net* for permission to reproduce excerpts from our first foray into writing collaboratively in this book.

We thank each other.

Contents

CHAPTER 1

Introduction

Critical Coordinates

In *The Interpretation of Dreams* (1900) Sigmund Freud establishes an analogous relationship between psychoanalysis and capitalism when, in an extended metaphor, he borrows from the language of finance to explain the role of the unconscious as a site of psychic production:

> A daytime thought may very well play the part of *entrepreneur* for a dream; but the *entrepreneur*, who, as people say, has the idea and the initiative to carry it out, can do nothing without capital; he needs a *capitalist* who can afford the outlay, and the capitalist who provides the psychical outlay for the dream is invariably and indisputably, whatever may be the thoughts of the previous day, *a wish from the unconscious.*[1]

Here Freud imagines the dream as requiring a form of seed capital or angel investment to realize its entrepreneurial ambitions, figuring the conscious and unconscious mind respectively as actors within a psychic economy. The unconscious acts as a reserve bankrolling the conscious mind, a speculative investment from which to gain future profit. In one of his 1913 'Papers on Technique', Freud again draws upon this conceptual vocabulary when he marks a symbolic association within bourgeois society between sexuality and the culture of capital:

M.-D. Dick, R. McLaughlan, *Late Capitalist Freud in Literary, Cultural, and Political Theory*,
https://doi.org/10.1007/978-3-030-47194-1_1

> He [the analyst] can point out that money matters are treated by civilized people in the same way as sexual matters—with the same inconsistency, prudishness and hypocrisy. The analyst is therefore determined from the first not to fall in with this attitude, but, in his dealings with his patients, to treat of money matters with the same matter-of-course frankness to which he wishes to educate them in things relating to sexual life. He shows them that he himself has cast off false shame on these topics, by voluntarily telling them the price at which he values his time.[2]

The logic of capitalist exchange that structures the psychoanalytic experience is further emphasized when Freud cautions against 'gratuitous treatments' on the basis that if money is psychically linked to repressed sexual urges, the prospect of a successful analysis is increased if the patient commits a financial investment in the process: '[f]ree treatment', Freud avers, 'enormously increases some of a neurotic's resistances'.[3] While the writing on technique and his emphasis on the expense of analysis is a marketing ploy of sorts, it also serves as a warning to any patient against undertaking a more affordable analysis at the hands of a less qualified analyst. The cost of Freudian analysis is a marker of its efficacy. Freud's use of the language of financial markets alludes to the imaginary of the bourgeois milieu to which he also makes appeal, gesturing to the implicit expectations of speculation and investment followed by accumulation and return, within the economy of psychoanalytic treatment itself. It also implies a deeper connection between psychoanalysis and the formation of capitalism in modernity; as conceptualized by Freud, psychoanalysis has always been implicated in the capitalist project.

Our book brings the writings of the late Freud into analysis with four crisis points of late capitalism: politics, technology, the body and culture. In it, we set out to address a question posed by Eli Zaretsky in the Afterword to his book *Political Freud: A History* (2015): '[i]s Freud's thought solely of historical interest, or is it relevant to our lives today?'.[4] To argue for a *Late Capitalist Freud* not only accepts the implicit challenge in Zaretsky's question to resist a historicizing of Freud—as if the age of Freud were over—but reveals the active influence that the late work continues to exert in understanding all aspects of our contemporary life. Contrary to the proclamations that psychoanalysis today is both an archaic and redundant science, we suggest that the scientific, clinical, therapeutic, or curative validity of psychoanalysis is irrelevant. Whether neuroscience disproves the existence of the unconscious (it hasn't) or MRI scanners can detect some area of the brain that functions analogously to the Freudian superego (it may have) is, we contend, completely immaterial to the continued significance of the late Freud's metapsychology in understanding contemporary late capitalist democracy. The 'Freud Wars' of the 1980s already proclaimed the death of psychoanalysis and the influence of Freudian theory at the turn of the previous century. H.J. Eysenck claimed that Freud's writing had evaded rigorous critical investigation largely because the 'camp-followers of the Freudian movement' had been myopic in their adherence to Freud's writing, such that works on Freud and psychoanalysis rejected all criticism as a form of ideological attack: 'they are therefore uncritical, unaware of alternative theories, and written more as weapons in a war of propaganda than objective assessments of the present status of psychoanalysis'.[5] More recently, the polemical findings presented in Frederick Crews's *Freud: The Making of an Illusion* (2017) rehearse Eysenck's criticisms of adherents of Freudian theory as too invested, both intellectually and financially, to realize the falsity of psychoanalysis. At the risk of interpellation into this critique, does it not gesture to the persistent vitality of Freudian thought, both in its perceived threat and its continued relevance to debate?.

Our argument has two central contentions. The first is that the 'social' turn by which the thought of the late Freud is critically characterized has, throughout the twentieth century and into the post-millennium, influenced how contemporary capitalist institutions understand their citizen-consumers. Our second and subsequent claim is that we might understand certain crisis points of contemporary late capitalism by examining them in parallel with the late Freudian writing, both in their formation through its influence and in how they testify to the broader sustainability of his theory on culture within democracy. There are two interrelated strands to this position. The first is the empirical claim, based on historical study, that Freud's metapsychology has made a central contribution to what Wendy Brown describes as 'neoliberal rationality', the mode by which neoliberalism goes beyond the financial sphere and becomes a governing political rationality that transforms by economizing all domains of contemporary life.[6] We examine how its adoption by the discursive practices of advertising, marketing, industrial administration and government connect Freudian cultural psychology to mid twentieth-century liberal democracy and its later formation in a contemporary late capitalist free-market economy. The second strand contends the value of the social theories of the late Freud to interpreting late capitalism, premised both on the empirical argument for the cultural influence of that theory and on a theoretical analysis of its principles as they have been realized and can be discerned within contemporary life. We are suggesting that concepts established in the late Freudian canon can be recognized in aspects of twenty-first century cultural and political institutions, and that their presence demonstrates both the afterlife of Freudian theory as it has been consciously dispersed into the cultural sphere, *and* the lived substantiation of Freudian thought within the late writing as it pertains to his theories on the individual within society.

We wish to distinguish between the circularity that might be inherent to using Freud to interrogate a world that we claim has been shaped by Freud and the alternative position that we are outlining here. Our argument proposes both that Freudian theory has had a historical influence on the configuration of contemporary life—in forming understandings of mass democracy, of the figure of the leader and of the role of institutions in regulating social control—and also that we can discern the broader realization of certain concepts within the late Freudian corpus as they are borne out by particular manifestations of late capitalist culture. As such, we maintain the historical importance of Freudian thought in all its dimensions: as it has been used and adapted within society; in its value as an interpretative model to understanding society thus influenced; and in the theoretical significance we claim for it to a comprehension of contemporary neoliberal existence. We assess the contribution that a historical and theoretical consideration of the late Freud might make to analyzing certain crisis points of late capital, arguing that concepts deployed within the late Freudian writing to theorize society are borne out and substantiated in the ontological shift in the human subject and democratic imaginary that Brown contends is pursuant on the socio-economic development of neoliberalism.

Contrary to the proclamations of Eysenck, Crews et al., we argue that we continue to exist in the shadow of the Freudian Empire and to live in the long Freudian century. In order to understand the so-called crisis in liberal democracy in the geopolitical west—signified across phenomena of populist revolts, financial instability, technological subsumption and an epidemic of mental health disorders—we return to the work produced by Freud in the final years of his life.[7] This book maps how psychoanalytic theories gave shape to the system of capitalist democracy that defined the previous century; yet it is not simply an intellectual historiography that recounts the importance of Freudian ideas to the expansion of a capital model, but an attempt to articulate how, long after its supposed demise, Freudian theory continues to be one of the most important conceptual systems we possess to expose and analyze the workings of capitalism today.

Following the Freud wars of the 1980s, which marked a societal and scientific turning away from Freud and its replacement with emergent neuro-technologies, there has been a recent resurgence of critical attention to psychoanalysis and psychoanalytic history. Succeeding Peter Gay's classic 1988 biography *Freud: A Life for Our Time*, Joel Whitebook's *Freud: An Intellectual Biography* (2017) has opened up Freudian theory to recent developments in gender theory, examining the relationship of Freud to his own mother Amalia, whom Whitebook speculates suffered from depression, to elucidate the origins of Freud's interest in familial psychodynamics.[8] Élisabeth Roudinesco followed her 1999 biography of Jacques Lacan with *Freud: In His Time and Ours* (2014), casting light on Freud's sexual conservatism in his personal life and forensically scrutinizing his early refusal to fully acknowledge the threat posed by National Socialism.[9] More than any other biography of Freud, Roudinesco's study marks and stresses a change in Freud's disposition after the end of war in Europe, his writing reflecting a dark turn towards ideas of the Occult, the uncanny and death. Even Frederick Crews, the arch critic of Freud and psychoanalysis today, has entered the fray. His *Freud: The Making of an Illusion* (2017) sets out to dismantle the image of Freud as 'the all-daring, all-risking hero or villain that he has sometimes been taken to be', and represents an extended biography of Freud's early years in Vienna.[10] For Crews, 'Freudolatry' in the Arts and Humanities elides and masks the discredited status that he holds in the sciences.[11]

Roudinesco's discernment of a shift in tone in Freud's correspondence and writing after 1918 accords with an established scholarly demarcation of the late work as exhibiting an increasingly pessimistic strain as it moves towards a metapsychology of society. Extending from biography, critical studies on psychoanalysis have also refocused on the late Freudian corpus. Todd Dufresne's *The Late Sigmund Freud: Or, the Last Word on Psychoanalysis, Society, and All the Riddles of Life* (2017) focuses on this period to make the case that the cultural writing produced in the final years of Freud's life is defined by the theories presented in *Beyond the Pleasure Principle* (1920), arguing that, despite received opinion, the final works are not merely supplemental within the canon but the place where its full scope is realized. Dufresne concentrates on *The Future of an Illusion* (1927), *Civilization and its Discontents* (1930) and *Moses and Monotheism*

(1939) to emphasize the importance of the theory of death drive as its development casts a haunting shadow over the work produced in the final decades of Freud's life. Disrupting a popular image that imagines Freud as the committed empiricist and Carl Gustav Jung as distracted by occultic flights of fancy, he reads *Beyond the Pleasure Principle* not only as the seminal work of the period, but as a 'ghost story', its focus on death, repetition and death drive representing 'the pinnacle of occult research'.[12] *The Late Sigmund Freud* locates the continued significance of Freud firmly in the realm of the philosophical as 'a fascinatingly baroque attempt to translate Romanticism' into the language of science; like Crews, Dufresne ultimately conceives of psychoanalysis as a now debunked science, observing that 'the privilege of retrospection permits a harsh verdict on Freud's own terms: it belongs entirely to the history of wishful thinking, illusion, and mass delusion'.[13]

There has also been a distinct re-emergence of a Freudo-Marxist paradigm, and a critical focus on the relationship between psychoanalysis and capitalism more broadly. Beyond the Ljubljana School, which has popularized a synthesis of theory that melds together predominantly Lacanian psychoanalysis with Marxist political philosophy, recent works including Todd McGowan's *Capitalism and Desire: The Psychic Cost of Free Markets* (2016) and Eli Zaretsky's *Political Freud: A History* (2015) have approached late capitalism through the prism of Freud. Now an affiliate of the Ljubljana Lacanian-Marxists, McGowan provides a theoretical investigation into the relationship between capital and desire, as emblematized in what he identifies as the central paradox at the heart of contemporary capitalism: that subjects 'cling tightly to their dissatisfaction' even when it is this dissatisfaction that is 'holding them to capitalism'.[14] McGowan proposes that capitalism incorporates a psychoanalytic understanding of loss and lack into its very structuration, and that this reliance on lack is determined in the logic that governs the value commodities acquire within our culture. His argument suggests that commodities possess an illusory promise that can never be fully realized, mobilizing a chain of commodity fetishization propelled by unconscious desire, and posits that this incessant desire for gratification from commodity culture functions as the secular equivalent of the role that the holy (couched in Lacanian terms of the Big-Other) once occupied.

Our book is positioned within this identification of psychoanalysis and capitalism, aligned with the claim of Samo Tomšič's *The Capitalist Unconscious: Marx and Lacan* (2015) that psychoanalysis 'epistemologically and politically speaking' can offer a 'critical insight into the production of the capitalist subject'.[15] He identifies the politically ambivalent position that psychoanalysis occupies in contemporary political discourse, as for 'leftists all psychoanalysis does is normalise' while for 'neoliberals it never normalises enough and therefore should be abolished'.[16] Tomšič reconciles and evinces the importance of Marx's work to the thinking of the self-declared liberal Lacan, in the context of an innovative reading of *The Interpretation of Dreams* in terms of Marxian theory of labor value. Complicating the simplicity of Freud's conviction that all dreams represent a form of wish fulfilment by revealing the processes of psychic production behind the creation of dreams, its importance to contemporary psychoanalytic theory lies in his original reading of Freud's phrase *Traumarbeit* (dream work), to place greater emphasis on the way in which dreams are manufactured by unseen processes of condensation and/or displacement by the unconscious. For Tomšič wishes are a form of unconscious production that allow for a 'labour theory of the unconscious' to be proposed.[17]

We here follow within and bring together these two critical trends by suggesting that our understanding of psychoanalysis as it relates to the subject under late capitalism can be developed via a focus on the late writings of Freud's corpus, which we define as dating from the post-war period comprising the final two decades of his life. In *An Autobiographical Study* (1925) Freud demarcates 'the history of psycho-analysis [...] into two phases', delineating the first half of his career as work undertaken single-handedly—'I stood alone and had to do all the work myself'—and a later stage in which he worked as part of a psychoanalytic community of students and collaborators.[18] Freud's own conceptualization of psychoanalysis invites a reading of the distinctions that appear and the detours that he makes in his later work via his framework of early/isolated and late/collaborative. This isolated/collaborative model, however, fails to accommodate the change in style and theoretical focus that has led to the late work being characterized by a dual shift towards tonal pessimism and a conceptual turn away from the psyche of the individual towards the proposition of a cultural psyche. Following this line of interpretation, the early dream work outlined in *The Interpretation of Dreams* and the parapraxis of *The Psychopathology of Everyday Life* express an optimism that is absent in the later work. Whether Freud in his early years was ever inclined to levity—despite a renowned appreciation for cocaine—the barbarism of war, of which he had experience through correspondence with his sons Martin and Ernst, who were engaged in active combat, together with the onset of the oral cancer that would lead to thirty-three operations and culminate in the surgical removal of his hard palate had inevitably exacted their toll in later life.[19] The last fifteen years of Freud's life were marked by ever-present forms of suffering; from the death of his 'Sunday-Child' Sophie in 1920 to the oral prosthesis he was forced to wear and that would chafe and make talking difficult, the later Freud was a figure who had grown accustomed to pain. The distress he experienced coincides in the late work with an increasing skepticism, linked to a redirection of his diagnostic focus away from the individual to a study of the masses within civilization.[20]

The so-called social, cultural, political or sociological turn in Freud has become established as an epochal marker by which to differentiate the later work from Freud's earlier publications, and this book agrees with that model to a certain extent. Freud himself was obviously aware of a change in his psychoanalytic attention away from the 'patient observation' towards what he refers to in *An Autobiographical Study* as forms of social 'speculation'; yet such a framework, dividing the clinical from the social, elides the omnipresent importance of the social as evinced by the emphasis that Freud places on the individual *within* society from the early writing and throughout his corpus.[21] In a paper from 1913 entitled 'The Claims of Psycho-Analysis to Scientific Interest' Freud observes that it 'is true that psycho-analysis has taken the individual mind as its subject, but in investigating the individual it could not avoid dealing with the emotional basis of the relation of the individual to society'.[22] It is undeniable that his later writings evidence a more sophisticated understanding of the psychic life of an individual within society as he works to further explicate the repressive role that the external world, as structured by the reality principle, plays in the frustration of innate drives; however, Freud's earliest work displays an enduring concern with assimilating patients into the dominant social logic of everyday life.[23] Within this finer distinction, we maintain a broad agreement with the clear change demarcated between the early work as it is concerned with the individual in society and the late work which moves towards a psychology of culture, according with that wider shift while emphasizing that because individual psychology always has a social dimension for Freud, the movement should be construed as a continuum of changing emphasis rather than an epochal break.

Within our chronology of late Freud, we consider the classical texts *Beyond the Pleasure Principle* (1920), *Group Psychology and the Analysis of the Ego* (1921), and *Civilization and Its Discontents* (1930) and revisit work that remains under-studied in psychoanalytic criticism and critical theory: 'The Claims of Psycho-Analysis to Scientific Interest' (1913); *On Narcissism* (1914); *The Ego and the Id* (1923); *An Autobiographical Study* (1925); 'Neurosis and Psychosis' (1924); 'The Loss of Reality in Neurosis and Psychosis' (1924); *The Future of an Illusion* (1927); *Why War?* (1933); *New Introductory Lectures on Psycho-Analysis* (1933); 'Constructions in Analysis' (1937); *Analysis Terminable and Interminable* (1937); and *An Outline of Psycho-Analysis* (1940). As we situate these within the context of contemporary neoliberalism, we take our primary coordinate from Fredric Jameson's seminal definition of late capitalism as it emerged from that of the Frankfurt School and advanced in the post-World War II era, developing out of post-Fordism and an industrial capitalism marked by economic expansionism and mass consumption. Jameson's definition emphasizes the coincidence of the economic structuration of late capitalism with postmodernism, so that from the 1970s onwards late capitalism assumes the aspect of a world system wherein culture and economics are assimilated, and subjects subsumed to its totalization. In this new formation it accrues further valences through the advent of finance capital in the 1980s, defined by the dominance of the free-market model, globalized flows of multinational capital and a mediascape wherein information proliferates and capitalist values are reproduced.[24] We are specifically concerned with late capitalism as it has become identified with neoliberalism, the economic ideology that both David Harvey and Wendy Brown categorize as a political project.[25] Brown observes that the term is a 'loose and shifting signifier'; there are variations in whether it is viewed as economic policy, order of reason, or mode of governance, as well as differing geographical and historical manifestations of its practice.[26] We adhere here to the lineage of its emergence from the Mont Pelerin Society as a reaction to Keynesian economic planning, and the establishment from the 1970s onwards of politico-economic policy situated in laissez-faire liberalism that promoted deregulation and privatization in the service of a move away from the state towards globalized free markets and labor forces, facilitated by technology. We are concerned with its contemporary manifestation under finance capitalism and its more recent iteration, austerity capitalism, which has been concurrent with the onset of the information age.

Within this designation our key model is taken from Wendy Brown, whose examination of the specific historical markers that neoliberalism has attained in its contemporary mode argues that it has become a political modality of governance—the organization of social conduct—and that this transformation is key to its new ability to economize all spheres of life, beyond those that are directly economic.[27] For Brown, ontology is altered under contemporary neoliberalism as it 'transmogrifies every human domain and endeavor, along with humans themselves, according to a specific image of the economic'. Within this framework, the objective is to enhance our capital value, measured according to a metric model.[28] It follows that neoliberal rationality evacuates democracy, replacing collective rule with atomized human capital and political principles with an order of governance derived from the economic.[29]

Within these critical fields, we position this book in alignment with the returned interest in psychoanalysis and capitalism, intersecting with a nascent interest in the late work of Freud, and in the context of studies of neoliberalism within contemporary culture. Our analysis focuses these critical coordinates around four key 'crises' in late capitalism, each of which comprises a chapter of this study. Chapter 2, 'A Politics of Freud', traces the political turn in the late Freud by reading *The Future of an Illusion* and *Why War?* as representative of Freud's theoretical move away from the clinical towards the social. This chapter examines the social, cultural and ideological afterlife of the late Freud's political turn, in which his work can be characterized by an increased pessimism that culminates in his proposal for the establishment of a secular 'dictatorship of reason'. This model of a rational elite formed from the middle classes emerged as the dominant form of social organization in the twentieth century, and we argue that the recent 'crises in democracy' are a reaction against Freud's demand for a rule by educated technocracies. This chapter explains the rise of both Donald Trump and other anti-establishment political movements as developments that have, unwittingly, revealed the extent to which Freud's model of a 'dictatorship of reason' has resulted in modern society being experienced by multiform constituencies of voters as a regime of repression. Our reading analyzes the comments made by then candidate-elect Donald Trump on *Access Hollywood* and his subsequent defense of 'locker room talk' to suggest how the voting booth might function as a psychic extension of the locker room, providing an ostensibly cathartic space for individuals to express a latent collective frustration with the perceived repressions of contemporary everyday life.

Our third chapter, '(Psycho) Social Media', follows the rise of Silicon Valley, showing how digital social networks and so-called disruptive technologies are underpinned by a psychoanalytic understanding of the lives of users, enabling a fusion of the digital and the logic of the market.

Increasingly, and as demonstrated by the recent Cambridge Analytica scandal, their operations are seen to accelerate beyond the law and to be outside of national jurisdictions. This chapter discusses the ontological influence of social media, arguing that our online presence on platforms such as Twitter, Instagram and Facebook constitutes an evolution of the Freudian superego that we term the cyber superego. We propose that social networks manifest the psychoanalytic importance of the role of desire within contemporary life and demonstrate how it can be manipulated in the pursuit of power. Chapter 4, 'Bodily Economies' asks how we perform as human capital within contemporary capital and conceives the body as an economy within which wider economies, both financial and psychic, intersect. It focuses on the recent trend towards wellness as a post-millennial, secular belief system that revolves around the ritual and rhetoric of self-care, a phenomenon that transfers the vocabulary of corporate finance to conceptions of individual wellbeing. Mapping the movement from a Foucauldian 'care of the self' towards a neoliberal, reflexive, self-care, we argue that the body-ego and ego-ideal initiate a trend for an ostensibly holistic approach to the mind-body paradigm of wellness. This chapter analyzes how leisure becomes the site of labor, via a study of late Freudian social thinking as developed through Herbert Marcuse. Our fifth chapter, 'Culture in the Age of Death Drive', discusses the Freudian term *kultur* as it relates to forms of cultural production. Freud's theorizing of death drive posed critical problems for the psychoanalytic project; this chapter examines how culture mediates between the destructive desires of the citizen-subject and the society that they inhabit. We extend the term 'culture' to read psychoanalysis itself as a 'a work of culture', the designation given to it by Freud and that would direct the psychoanalytic project in his absence, ultimately leading to the expulsion of Lacan from the International Psychoanalytical Association (IPA) on the grounds of his alleged theoretical heresy. Our final section develops these dual understandings of culture to consider contemporary production in late capital and its illumination of the architecture of restriction upon the individual, in light of Freud's theorizing of death drive.

In a passage from *Civilization and Its Discontents* to which we will return to in the next chapter, Freud speculates that:

> The super-ego of an epoch of civilization has an origin similar to that of an individual. It is based on the impression left behind by the personalities of great leaders—men of overwhelming force of mind or men in whom one of

> the human impulsions has found its strongest and purest, and therefore often its most one-sided, expression.[30]

This explanation for the emergence of charismatic leaders analyzes the imprint of their psychology upon the wider socio-cultural terrain to form a zeitgeist; while it can be used to understand the following that modern political leaders accrue or indeed encourage, we wish here to refocus critical attention away from political leaders who occupy a global stage and onto cultural formations and figures, whom we propose as case studies through which to chart the role of psychoanalysis in the historical development of twentieth-century capitalism. In this, we accord with Eli Zaretsky's assessment that Freud offers a route to comprehending the century, both as psychoanalytic history interacts with and was in some cases co-opted to the grand narratives of the period—anti-Semitism, war, the sexual revolution—and as it contributes to its major liberatory movements:

> Freudian thought was integral to many if not all of the great progressive movements of the twentieth century, including the cultural rebellions of the 1920s, African American radicalism, surrealism, Popular Front antifascism, the New Left, radical feminism, and queer theory.[31]

By focusing on key points in the evolution of Freud's work as a form of mass psychology in the mid twentieth century, the second and third sections of our introduction constitute a contextual bridge to the twenty-first century focus of the following chapters. Spanning distinct but overlapping spaces of contemporary life, from Madison Avenue to an anti-psychiatry clinic in Scotland, it maps a period in which Freudian thought leaves the couch and takes to the streets and charts a genealogy of commercial and state-endorsed implementations of psychoanalytic models.

Freud in the Factory

We begin by assessing the legacy of a Freudian who reinvented the workplace in the early part of the last century, Elton Mayo, whose influence survives today in what has become a staple of every office environment across the world: the annual performance review. The mechanization of the labor market during the nineteenth century, which meant that commodities could now be produced at speed and on a scale hitherto impossible, coincided with a sustained period of population growth that conveniently provided new markets for capitalist expansion. Yet in the early decades of the new century markets began to slow as new middle-class consumers, content with their situations, withdrew from the financial network of commodity exchange. This posed a problem for producers who, now faced with the problem of how to move their goods, turned towards the ideas of psychoanalysis that were filtering into the Anglo-American public consciousness from Europe. As advertisers and producers came to apprehend how feelings of desire and lack might be exploited to manipulate the consumer unconscious, Freud's schematization of the subject as one who possessed unconscious desires, incapable of full satisfaction within society, was imperative to propelling a new era of mass consumption.

The role of Freud's nephew Edward Bernays in the evolution of capitalism from a nineteenth-century model of production to a twentieth-century model of consumption has been well documented elsewhere: the father of what we now know as public relations, present at the signing of the Treaty of Versailles, and responsible for popularizing the term 'banana republic'.[32] Bernays was the first to comprehend how the Freudian ideas he had gleaned from his reading of Uncle Sigmund's *New Introductory Lectures* might be used to manipulate the psychology of masses on an industrial scale, a theory he implemented to shape attitudes through propaganda when hired to work during the war for the US Government on the Committee on Public Affairs. Bernays then moved to what he considered the more expansive realms of public organization and consumer opinion, advising national governments, election candidates, politicians and blue-chip companies on how to create and manage a brand through the deployment of psychological techniques and institution of cultural myths into which the public would be induced to invest. In the evocatively titled *Propaganda* (1928), Bernays intimates how his Uncle's radical psychology might be utilized when he observes that men 'are rarely aware of the real reasons which motivate their actions', a fact as 'true of mass as of individual psychology'.[33] In an era of capitalist over-production, Bernays understood that public relations could guide corporations on how to appeal to the unconscious desires of consumers on a mass scale. He directly appeals to government and industry to rethink their approach to the masses, urging them towards a psychoanalytic conceptualization of society that would uncover the importance of human psychology to shaping material outcomes:

> An engineer may know all about the cylinders and pistons of a locomotive, but unless he knows how steam behaves under pressure he cannot make his engine run. Human desires are the steam which makes the social machine work. Only by understanding them can the propagandist control the vast, loose-jointed mechanism which is modern society.[34]

The mechanical metaphor of a society powered by mass desire implies that American financial and political imperialism would only be possible under the auspices of the Freudian Empire. Zaretsky draws from the import of Bernays when he proposes that psychoanalysis in the era of consumption should be understood as the twentieth-century equivalent of Max Weber's paradigm of a Calvinist 'spirit of capitalism'; nominating it as an intellectual driving force of the new formation, Zaretsky declares that 'psychoanalysis helped change the way in which capitalism was understood, from a mode of production to a mode of distribution and consumption'.[35]

While Bernays was transforming American culture into one of mass distribution and consumption, an Australian psychotherapist, Elton Mayo, had realized the significance of Freudian ideas to enacting a transformation in the workplace. Perhaps the most influential twentieth-century figure of whom no-one has heard beyond the world of corporate psychology, his synthesis of psychoanalysis with the sociology of Émile Durkheim was instrumental in developing a discipline that would be mobilized to understand the emerging labor economy of the early twentieth century. Industrial-organizational Psychology (I/O), an attempt to understand the human element in productive systems that were becoming increasingly mechanized, laid the foundations of the human relations industry; as with Bernays's public relations, many of its foundational insights came from the war economy, though it had first emerged in Germany in the early 1880s. Mayo's insight lay in his understanding of the applicability of Freud's psychosocial work to the organizational and industrial theory of American industry, and his turn to Freud would play an integral part in the advent of the second industrial revolution in the early decades of the twentieth century. After the war, American corporations became interested in using I/O as an organizational system to boost the productivity of workers; where Bernays possessed a macro interest in individuals as consumers and voters, Mayo focused on the emotional and psychological lives of American workers within their homes. In 1933, Mayo, who had first encountered Freud at University and would spend the rest of his life as a practicing psychotherapist, published *The Human Problems of an Industrial*

Civilization. The book described the results of the Hawthorne experiments on productivity at the Western Electric Factory in Chicago and would go on to have a profound impact on American labor relations. By transposing Freudian theory to the social life of workers, Mayo instigated a development in how the place of work is understood beyond the parameters of its office walls and factory floors.

Though Freud had introduced a new sexual vocabulary into modern American life, Bernays and Mayo recognized how Freudian theory could be utilized to understand and to influence every aspect of a wage worker's existence. In line with the late Freud's concentration on the individual within society, Mayo understood American workers as actors inhabiting a number of social networks, familial, professional and romantic, and civilization as a mesh of interpersonal relationships. Society, as understood by Mayo, 'is a group of families living in an ordered relation with each other'.[36] Mayo's investigations into the closed world of American domesticity revealed that American capitalism invested subjects with a dual economic importance as both worker and consumer, and that this double investment had implications for American democracy and capitalist society.[37] *The Human Problems of an Industrial Civilization* presents a capitalist vision of a utopian society functioning in a state of perfect equilibrium, an organized society; in contrast, a disorganized society is one in which individuals feel alienated from themselves, from their co-workers and, crucially, from the apparatus of the state. At the time of his writing, Mayo considered America to be a disorganized society by virtue of the dramatic redrawing of social relations that had accompanied the expansion of the American industrial economy, as American corporations were undergoing a transformative change away from the rigid hierarchies of the nineteenth century to a more bureaucratized structure of CEOs and line managers. The property owner, retaining the means of production for himself, had been replaced by the figure of the manager within a larger corporate system, so that, while capitalism had restructured social relations between workers and employers, it had also created a new dynamic between the bourgeoisie and proletariat.

Mayo, who like Bernays was wary of the socialist experiment underway in the Soviet Union, sought recourse to psychoanalysis to investigate the psychosocial consequences of urban industrialization at the level of the individual and the state. The rapid development of industrial technologies that promoted a disorganizing effect on a population had also affected the social landscape of industrialized nations:

> The consequence is that the imposition of highly systematized industrial procedures upon all the civilized cultures has brought to relative annihilation the cultural traditions of work and craftsmanship. Simultaneously the development of a higher labor mobility and a clash of cultures has seriously damaged the traditional routine of intimate and family life in the United States. Generally the effect has been to induce everywhere a considerable degree of social disorganization.[38]

The Human Problems of an Industrial Civilization also outlines the psychological experiments undertaken on behalf of large corporations, one of which in particular has left an indelible mark of influence on US labor practices as they survive today. In the 1920s, Mayo and a team of researchers from Harvard University began observing the workers of Western Electric for a group of workplace experiments that would eventually become known as the Hawthorne studies. Henry Ford's manufacturing line had resulted in his becoming one of the richest men in the world, but Fordism as a corporate strategy was physically and psychologically exhausting for the workers at the Ford Motor Company, and the researchers were interested in studying how variable external conditions might lead to a rise in productivity in mechanized labor. Although paying way above the average wage for the time, Ford was continuously blighted with a turn-over of staff estimated to be around 400%, meaning it was recruiting four people for one post every calendar year. The researchers sought to understand whether external conditions could have a direct impact on the productivity and the emotional satisfaction of workers engaged in the most monotonous form of labor. The premise of the experiment was simple: lighting in two rooms within the Western Electric factory was to be altered during various points of a worker's shift, the hypothesis being that productivity was expected to increase in the room illuminated brightly and decrease in the room that was darker. The results, however, did not align with researchers' expectations. To their surprise, they discovered no diminution of productivity in the darker room and no increase in enterprise in the brightly lit room; in fact, productivity seemed to have increased in both rooms, irrespective of the lighting conditions. The research team decided to repeat the experiment again: not only were the results replicated, but they noticed an increase in worker productivity for the entire duration they were based in the factory undertaking the experiment.

The Hawthorne researchers eventually concluded that this spike in efficiency was caused by a sense of pride among the factory workers, who felt flattered that their work was deemed of interest to researchers from Harvard University. The rise in productivity proved to be temporary as when the workers became accustomed to monitoring, productivity resorted back to pre-experiment levels. The spike was christened the Hawthorne effect, and Elton Mayo became increasingly interested in how the results hinted towards a psychological complexity on the part of workers. For Mayo, the contradictory results yielded by the experiment indicated that '[s]omehow or other that complex of mutually dependent factors, the human organism, shifted its equilibrium and unintentionally defeated the purpose of the experiment'.[39] As the workers were either consciously or unconsciously reacting to the attention paid to them by the researchers, this appeared to reveal an affective component in labor that had implications for productivity. Faithful to his Freudian training, Mayo interpreted the results as demonstrating a psychological response to work that warranted further psychological investigation.

One of the experiments designed by Mayo was culled directly from psychoanalysis. Mayo invited workers to speak freely about their experience of working in the factory; these interviews were initially undertaken by his team of researchers, who were later replaced by figures of managerial responsibility and prestige. Although workplace interviews were unheard of in the mechanized factories of American capitalism, Mayo argued that such practices had been long established in the psychoanalytic community: '[i]ts origins traced to clinical medicine; the Salpêtrière Hospital in Paris had developed it in the study of disordered mentalities; Vienna and Zurich had carried elaboration to the highest power'.[40] Mayo discovered that the importation of a Freudian method, designed to break the silence characterizing the asymmetrical power dynamics structuring the factory by encouraging workers to free associate on their working life, had a concomitant effect on morale and sense of professional pride. When workers were encouraged by those in professional authority to speak about their feelings towards their work, it was found that feelings of happiness and contentment rose proportionally. This increase in happiness, directly leading to an increase in productivity, was not quite as unambiguous as at first it seemed. Mayo's study revealed that it was insufficient simply to invite workers to free associate about their emotional responses to work and their experiences of being in the workplace but that, like all good psychoanalysts, the listener had to be adequately trained to make sense of the responses. Mayo had effectively invented a process that would evolve to become a feature of all corporate bodies in the neoliberal workplace:

the progress review. Contemporary corporate practices have their origins in Mayo's appeal for the mass training of an administrative elite, able to understand the language of a new working class and to make the necessary adjustments to their working lives; increasingly, this managerial class would mediate neoliberal values through the workplace by ventriloquizing a language created for its dissemination. Like Bernays, Mayo recognized that the implementation of Freud's ideas as corporate strategies possessed transformative possibilities: '[t]he world over we are greatly in need of an administrative *élite* who can assess and handle the concrete difficulties of human collaboration'.[41]

Mayo believed that whichever nation became the first to adopt this psychoanalytic methodology in order to understand the emotional complexity of its citizens would 'infallibly outstrip the others in the race for stability, security, and development'.[42] A conservative who believed in the social and psychological advantages of capitalism, Mayo advocated for captains of American industry to adopt a psychoanalytic understanding of listening in order to cultivate greater productivity, but also called for a similar strategy to be implemented at the level of government, maintaining that in order for the West to stave off the threat of the Soviet Union, it had to train and set free an army of administrators educated in Freudian psychoanalysis. The final chapter of *The Human Problems of an Industrial Civilization* reads as a direct appeal to government bureaucrats to make use of universities to train a listening elite to be deployed throughout all areas of American life. Trained listening on the part of the analyst was a crucial element in the famous 'talking cure' of psychoanalysis; however, once this was implemented and weaponized as a strategy of power, it would be transformed into a repressive tool which legitimized an era of mass state surveillance. The consequences of Mayo's theory of a listening elite were to be grave both for those citizens living in the supposed 'Land of the Free' and for the reputation of Freud, generating a reactionary movement cynical as to how psychoanalysis was being manipulated in order to foster new forms of social obedience, but which would, in turn, instigate a further evolution in Freudian theory.

Lobotomized Happiness

If the legitimacy of psychoanalysis and of Freud himself had been contested since its inception, it was subjected to a key re-evaluation in the mid twentieth century by the coalescence of medical practitioners, clinicians, writers and philosophers forming an alliance that became known as the anti-psychiatry movement. Influenced by the work of the Frankfurt School, the anti-psychiatry movement argued that Freudian psychoanalysis had been adopted by a ruling elite as a form of mass psychology, in a recognition both of the transformative impact that its appropriation by Bernays, Mayo and others had exerted upon American society and of what anti-psychiatry perceived to be a pathologizing of non-normativity to bring difference within the structures of the state. The most seditious figure from the early period of psychoanalysis was the Austrian-born Wilhelm Reich, who began his career as part of a brilliant second generation of psychoanalytic practitioners, before being formally expelled from the psychoanalytic community for the work that founded the Freudo-Marxist position. While Bernays and Mayo were interested in the application of Freudian group psychology to mass democracy, Reich's work issued a warning against the totalitarian ends of its implications, one that would be taken up by the anti-psychiatry movement as it sought to separate the individual from the state. Reich's interest in sexuality and the unconscious began in 1919, when he attended a lecture on psychoanalysis as a student. Although an often skeptical reader of Freud—his work on the therapeutic and emancipatory potential of sexual orgasms was especially challenging for the more loyal adherents of Freudianism—Reich's career in psychoanalysis was terminated in 1934, one year after the publication of *The Mass Psychology of Fascism* (1933), a work that would not only shape the philosophy of the Frankfurt School but also the anti-Freudianism of the anti-psychiatry movement.

Although writing against a brand of Marxism deemed 'vulgar' throughout the work, *The Mass Psychology of Fascism* begins from the classical Marxist position that the social prominence of those who own the means of production permits them to set the moral character of a society. Reich observed that the dominant ideology of an economic social order 'has the function not only of reflecting the economic process of this society, but also and more significantly of embedding this economic process in the *psychic structures of the people who make up the society*'.[43] Reich argues against a simplistic analysis of the masses as duped or corrupted by totalitarian systems of thought, a viewpoint that negates what he considered the socio-psychological dimension latent within all totalizing power structures. To prove his analysis, he encourages his reader to consider the following thought experiment:

> what has to be explained is not the fact that the man who is hungry steals or the fact that the man who is exploited strikes, but why the majority of those who are hungry *don't* steal and why the majority of those who are exploited *don't* strike.[44]

The answer for Reich was to be found in a Freudian understanding of the psychosexual and psychosocial development of children and how such processes are integral to the maintenance of hegemonic ideology. Reich's hypothetical challenge reveals how authoritarian power exploits the unconscious lives of citizens to cultivate absolute obedience, even when the logical or ethical response would be to rebel against moral imperatives prohibiting theft or civil disobedience. Freud's theory of civilization mandated that sexual desire be re-cathected into socio-cultural structures, a process termed 'sublimation', but Reich was unequivocal in his denunciation of this sacrifice of innate desire to the strictures of culture. From Marx, he realized that the owners of the means of production set the moral standards within society, but from his psychoanalytic training Reich determined that Freudian analysis was invested in sustaining repressive morality. In the insistence on social order that formed part of the political turn in Freud, Reich discerned the future encoding of a totalitarian state.

Reich was the first of Freud's critics to comprehend the social function that sexual repression plays in everyday life; *The Mass Psychology of Fascism* celebrates Freud for the 'devastating and revolutionary' impact that psychoanalysis had in establishing sexuality as present at the very beginning of a child's life.[45] If Freud was the great sexual revolutionary of his age, he was also, for Reich, the person responsible for demonstrating how libidinal desire had to be repressed in the interest of the greater social good. Freudian theory had proven that the dominant social 'moral code' is imparted to children during the Oedipal stage of development, during which parents are understood as the proxy representatives of an external reality who unconsciously demand that the 'laws of sexuality and of unconscious psychic life' are relinquished in favor of social structures that support 'sexual repression'.[46] Faithful to his Freudian credentials, Reich locates the source of sexual repression as originating from within the family home, but unlike Freud, who viewed the repression of Oedipal libidinality as a crucial step in a subject's psychosexual development towards maturation, Reich visualizes this injunction to repress sexual desire as the moment when a child becomes inducted into the dominant social ideology. Reich's critique of the family as a middle-class structure invested in the perpetuation of ideology not only brought him into direct conflict with the psychoanalytic community but would exert a lasting influence within the anti-psychiatry movement as it came into being later in the century:

> *The interlacing of the socio economic structure with the sexual structure of society and the structural reproduction of society take place in the first four or five years in the authoritarian family* [...] Thus, the authoritarian state gains an enormous interest in the authoritarian family: *It becomes the factory in which the state's structure and ideology are molded.*[47]

Reich later traveled to the United States, where he began his investigations into 'orgone' energy (a neologism combining 'organism' and 'orgiastic') and after a long dispute with the US Government was eventually imprisoned over the distribution of the 'Orgone accumulator', a box he believed could channel energy to destroy cancer. Nevertheless, his anti-Freudianism gathered momentum among a group of cultural figures that had started to emerge throughout American and European society, having developed a collective anger towards psychoanalysis and what they perceived to be its willing co-optation by the representatives of authority. In literature, Tennessee Williams, Arthur Miller and Ken Kesey had direct experience of the consequences attendant on the unquestioning faith of the general public for medical practitioners. In continental philosophy and psychotherapy, Michel Foucault, Gilles Deleuze and Félix Guattari included psychoanalysis in their critique of disciplinary society and capitalism; neo-Freudians including Bernays and Mayo, along with others working in the now-established field of Industrial Psychology, were targeted as representing the psychological wing of American capitalist culture. The Scottish psychiatrist R.D. Laing formed the third voice among an informal disciplinary triumvirate dedicated to exposing the responsibility borne by Freudian theory for an age of mass control, not only in the way it had been used by both the hospital and state to further medicalized and capitalist oppression, but for the inherent fascination for order maintained through repression that the anti-psychiatry movement detected within Freud's writing itself.

The problem with the talking cure was that a sense of cure was immanent to it, which the anti-psychiatry movement criticized as establishing a threshold of psychological normality indexed to productivity. The aim of analysis, and later of the pharmaceutical companies that monetized neurotic illness as the chemical heirs to Freud, was to therapize or medicate individuals back to work. Freud himself was more ambivalent on the end goal of psychoanalysis—it is never clear whether the talking cure was a cure at all—but the proponents of anti-psychiatry within philosophy charged that psychoanalysis removed the singularity of patients when transforming them into case histories or studies, and that it exercised a disciplinary function of normalizing citizens. As Freud writes in his 'Postscript' (1927) to *The Question of Lay Analysis* (1926), psychoanalysis created an 'inseparable bond between cure and research', and the accrual of '[k]nowledge brought therapeutic success'.[48] In *The Question of Lay Analysis*, he identifies the acquisition and dispensing of knowledge as both that which differentiates the psychoanalyst from the figure of the 'quack' and the source of the analyst's authority. The interest of psychoanalysis in the self-sustaining dyad of power and knowledge legitimized the effacement of the singularity of the individual in the creation of the patient as case study to be probed, measured, assessed and, ultimately, controlled.

Deleuze and Guattari extended this critique to the structural level of capitalism when in *Anti-Oedipus* (1972) they return to Reich's critique of psychoanalysis as an instrument of social exploitation, remarking that the 'astonishing thing is not that some people steal' but that 'all those who are starving do not steal as a regular practice'.[49] They discern a masochistic element to a subject's toil under the impossible labor demands and the iniquitous social relations brought about under capitalism: 'why do people still tolerate being humiliated and enslaved, to such a point, indeed, that they *actually want* humiliation and slavery not only for others but for themselves?'.[50] As Reich had shown in his study of fascism, the masses had not been deceived but instead inculcated through ideology into unconsciously adhering to totalitarianism as a social system; Deleuze and Guattari return to fascism to take a further theoretical step in associating its barbarism with the brutality of capitalism, going so far as to suggest that the masses masochistically craved their exploitation: 'at a certain point, under a certain set of conditions, they *wanted* fascism, and it is this perversion of the desire of the masses that needs to be accounted for'.[51] The psychosexual history of the subject as it is linked to its social formation was also emphasized by Foucault in his analysis of the hospital as a laboratory wherein the state can exercise its claims to absolute authority. The Freudian revolution in psychology had reconfigured the way that psychological illness was understood and engaged with; patients were to be released from the cells of the asylum and listened to in the wards of new hospitals but, instead of facilitating a similar revolution in psychiatric treatment, the development of psychoanalytic theory in the post-Freudian world had resulted in new repressive formations of surveillance and control. The hospital was not simply a gendered space—a micro version of capitalist patriarchy—but one governed by a logic that reflected the wider dictates of heteronormative familial life. The doctor accrued power within society because he represented the figure of the father, asserting the cultural significance accorded to fathers as it reflected their structuration of the psychosexual lives of children. Within a Freudian schema the Father, as in the foundational story of Oedipus's killing of his father, is the figure upon whom the child projects murderous feelings, having intuitively identified him as rival to the desired mother; in a later stage of psychosexual theory, the figure of the father becomes internalized within the psyche of the child: this figure of prohibition who prohibits the flow of maternal desire from the child is transformed and internalized into the superego within the structural model. Foucault's hospital space is populated by superego agents in possession of juridical authority to decide the appropriate behaviors, emotions and language of patients in line with a capitalist reality principle. His skepticism of psychoanalysis centers on its deployment within the clinic in the promotion of psychological conformity, eliding difference in favor of homogeneity; Foucault is not concerned with the validity of psychoanalysis as a therapeutic methodology but, like Reich, in how it had been pressed into the service of hegemonic power.

Foucault's critique of Freudian analysis was primarily shaped by the work of R.D. Laing, which came out of the Glasgow psychiatric hospitals of the early 1950s. The logic of the nineteenth-century asylum had been replaced with a new language to describe the etiological origins and distressing symptomology that Laing encountered on the wards, but he wondered why, given these twentieth-century claims to psychological enlightenment in the post-Freudian world, the patients under his care—the majority of whom were women—were not improving sufficiently to be allowed home. In *The Politics of Experience* (1967), Laing laid the groundwork for what he termed 'social phenomenology', essentially a mapping of the affective experience of everyday life. When he examined why his female patients would exhibit signs of improvement only to relapse back into depressive or anxious symptoms once returning home, the conclusion at which he arrived was a startling one: that modern life was experienced as both repressive and oppressive and that, behind the respectable front doors of a new suburbia, the private lives of women were being made intolerable by a patriarchal system that encouraged the repression of innate human instincts. The chief force in this system of repression was the family. As Marx had identified a century earlier, the bourgeois family unit served as a microcosm for a wider patriarchy, and it was an environment wherein men assumed absolute authority. Reich extended Marx's analysis of the family to attach a psychological importance to the role of the family unit in the replication of hegemonic ideology and had established the family as 'the authoritarian state in miniature, to which the child must learn to adapt himself as preparation for the general social adjustment required of him later'.[52] Organizational systems cultivated ideological servility by '*the embedding of sexual inhibitions and fear in the living substance of sexual impulses*'.[53] Laing shared this Reichian cynicism of the 'most important source for the reproduction of the authoritarian social system' in his work on the ideological value of the family within twentieth-century capitalism. Instead of providing a source of support, care and love, Laing argued that the traditional unit generated a sense of profound alienation among those unwilling or unable to conform to the dominant social ideology underpinning middle-class family life. Just as industrialization had alienated the worker from their labor and from themselves, Laing identified the family, with its rigid patrilineal structure, as the primal source of psychic trauma and repression. In the same way that Marx's factory worker internalized their oppression within the capitalist mode of production, female subjects were violently made to adhere within the home to the same patriarchal logic that governed the world beyond their front door. Laing's work revealed how the symbolic architecture of domestic spaces was organized to repress women; instead of providing a sense of familial security, it had become a microcosm of panoptic capitalist power, leading Laing to conclude that: '[t]he *family* as a *system* is internalised'.[54]

As children we invest in our parents an authority that lingers on throughout the course of our lives. Anti-psychiatry proponents stressed that psychoanalysis had not simply been taken over by the agents of oppression as a means to police, order and, ultimately, regulate society, but that Freud's political work, once realized, ends in repressive social organization. It was Freud, after all, who had stressed the primal importance of fathers in *Totem and Taboo* (1913), a strange text for its theorization that the origins of modern civilization are founded upon the patricidal murder of the primal father at the hands of his two sons. For Freud the historic killing doubles as the psychoanalytic version of the fall of man, the original moment in which guilt was released into the world. For Laing, the centrality of the male figure within twentieth-century life found an echo in the axial importance that Freud placed upon the figure of Father within his metapsychology.

The centrality of male figures of authority in psychoanalysis had, according to the anti-psychiatry movement, inadvertently led to the male doctor being imbued with a social value disproportionate to his training. This power became absolute when pressed into the service of the broader state apparatus. Anti-psychiatry had a celebrity example of the dangers of unregulated practice in the death of Marilyn Monroe, whose suicide had resulted in part from an unconventional psychiatric experiment under the American psychoanalyst Ralph Greenson that went catastrophically wrong. His analysis of Monroe involved moving her into the confines of the family home and casting himself as a proxy father figure, and its eventual consequences signified a further stigmatizing of psychoanalysis within the collective American imagination. In the aftermath of her death Monroe's ex-husband Arthur Miller gave voice to a collective discontent over how deregulated psychiatry had come to occupy a privileged space within American culture. He shared the concern of the anti-psychiatry movement that modern psychiatry had become obsessed with therapizing towards a threshold of psychological normality, understood by Miller as a form of state violence masked as medical altruism. Anyone deemed threatening to the dominant ideology was made to conform through the repressive state apparatus of psychiatry, leading Miller to question what was meant by American values of freedom and individualism in an age where the standard of psychological normality was set by a profession that effectively functioned as the medical wing of the State:

> My argument with so much of psychoanalysis, is the preconception that suffering is a mistake, or a sign of weakness, or a sign even of illness. When in fact, possibly the greatest truths we know, have come out of people's suffering. The problem is not to undo suffering, or to wipe it off the face of the earth, but to make it inform our lives, instead of trying to cure ourselves of it constantly, and avoid it, and avoid anything but that lobotomized sense of what they call happiness. There's too much of an attempt, it seems to me, to think in terms of controlling man, rather than freeing him, of defining him, rather than letting him go! It's part of the whole ideology of this age, which is power-mad![55]

Miller attacks psychoanalysis for severing the socio-historical relationship between reason and unreason. As the practice and influence of psychoanalysis had developed in the years following Freud's death, it had gained the reputation of an epistemology that legitimized forms of psychological apartheid. The anti-psychiatry movement criticized the adoption of psychoanalysis by ideologues as a form of mass psychology, in effect drawing attention to the way in which Freudian theories of the unconscious had been instilled as the primary means of understanding citizens. Under such a system of psychic control, all citizens were made to conform to an ideal of lobotomized happiness. In *Propaganda*, Bernays had shown how the 'intelligent manipulation' of the masses was not only possible, but that it represented 'an important element in democratic society', adding that those 'who manipulate this unseen mechanism of society constitute an invisible government which is the true ruling power of our country'.[56] Although the anti-psychiatry movement initiated a new era in the treatment of psychological conditions, their criticisms would prove to have a more sustained outcome. The anti-psychiatry dream of liberating the individual from state-enforced conformity resulted in a radical reconceptualizing of the relationship of the individual to society: if society was the etiological cause of psychological illness, then the solution was to liberate subjects from an identification with the masses. The summer of love, the Vietnam protests in 1967, and the student riots of 1968 represented a reaction against the oppressive nature of the state and the encroaching identification of culture with capital. Yet the countercultural exposure of Western professional and domestic life as the causation of a contemporary pandemic of neurotic disorders would itself instigate an evolution in the design of capitalism. Unbeknown to the philosophers, psychologists and artists of the counterculture, the revolution that they enacted would usher in a more absolutist form of capitalist oppression, one that would again be underpinned by the inheritance of Freud.

In their seminal investigation into what they conceive as the 'new spirit of capitalism', Luc Boltanski and Eve Chiapello acknowledge the importance of the anti-psychiatry ethos in the developmental history of twentieth-century capitalism. The anti-psychiatry movement's privileging of the individual and its promotion of spaces liberated from state surveillance led to a mutation in the architecture of capitalism but, crucially for Boltanksi and Chiapello, this evolution heralded the introduction of an even more insidious form of capitalist control. Like Vladimir Lenin, who declared to The Communist International of 1920 that with capitalism '[t]here is no such thing as an absolutely hopeless situation',[57] Boltanski and Chiapello identify as one of capitalism's defining characteristics the ability to rework and then incorporate any resistance that threatens its legitimacy or longevity: '[t]he capitalist system has proved infinitely more robust than its detractors—Marx at their head—thought. But this is also because it has discovered routes to its survival in critiques of it'.[58] Boltanski and Chiapello explain how mid twentieth-century critiques of capitalism inadvertently renewed the entire organizational system, as those seeking liberation from the oppressive injunctions of professional and personal life were rewarded by a new individualist ethos that would ultimately set subjects into opposition against each other in ever more aggressive ways. This mutation offered the apparent emancipation of individual desire, but within the strict framework of a Bernaysian vision of the masses as, in order for society to function and capitalism to continue to thrive, new demographics were constructed to allow a sense of individualism to find expression in a way that would benefit the entire social body. Influenced by Freud and the post-Freudians' work on mass psychology, the graduates of Business Degrees who had studied I/O before entering the workplace recuperated the impulse towards greater autonomy and reintegrated it within the conceptual design of the system. By creating precise demographic groupings, corporations were able to manufacture to consumers in ways hitherto not possible, so that even a grouping that was ostensibly subversive in its potential to remain outside market dictates—for example, hippies—could be assimilated into the free-market economy. This development of Bernays's desire economy was facilitated by Freudian principles of object cathexis, whereby the commodity becomes transformed, via unconscious desire, into a totemic object, in a process that recalls the famous dancing table from Marx's *Capital* (1867). The irony resulting from the zeitgeist that propelled the countercultural resistance to society was that its desire for individualist emancipation from the masses gave rise to further forms of disciplinary control and social alienation. Boltanski and Chiapello describe this as the paradox of a new individualism leading to a proliferation of the neurotic anxieties against which it was supposed to inoculate:

> far from finding themselves liberated, many people were instead casualized, subjected to new forms of systematic dependency, obliged to confront undefined, unlimited and distressing exigencies of self-fulfillment and autonomy in greater solitude, and, in most cases, separated from the lived

> world where nothing helped them to fulfil themselves. For many people, the development of these new forms of specific alienation thus cancelled out the 'generic' liberation that seemed to have been achieved.[59]

Although writing from a predominantly French socio-historical perspective, Boltanski and Chiapello's analysis draws attention to how an anti-Freudianism, arising from the anti-psychiatry movement as part of a broader awareness of—and revolt against—the manipulation of mass psychology, led to a nuancing of capitalist control:

> Thus [...] the qualities that are guarantees of success in this new spirit—autonomy, spontaneity, rhizomorphous capacity, multitasking [...] conviviality, openness to others and novelty, availability, creativity, visionary intuition, sensitivity to differences, listening to lived experience and receptiveness to a whole range of experiences, being attracted to informality and the search for interpersonal contacts—these are taken directly from the repertoire of May 1968.[60]

Post-1968, demographers effectively embarked on a project to map the population in order to design a structure capable of manipulating the unconscious desires of subjects with greater efficiency and expediency; the homogeneity of the mass was sub-divided into niche demographic clusters marked by identity characteristics that would enable them to be targeted in more sophisticated ways. In politics, this was achieved through a combination of a mass taxonomy of voters via focus groups, a further evolution of the talking cure; in advertising, a new wave of marketers emerged who promised to be able to tap into the unconscious through a renewal of Freudian theory. The act of listening underwent a parallel development in importance to the historiography of the modern subject under capital: from the adaptation of Freudian technique for Mayo's trained listeners to its implementation in hospital wards for the purpose of surveillance rather than cure, leading on to the formation of the focus group and its central place in advertising, politics and the workplace. Towards our contemporary period, the ability to target consumers algorithmically has resulted in bespoke advertising strategies tailored to individual desire as expressed through the search engine. The vision of the subject emerging from critiques of Freud, focused on a mistrust of the family as a closed social system and on wider skepticism of the use of mass and individual psychology within democracy, contributed to the emergent sovereignty of the individual as subject and consumer in the final decades of the twentieth century. Further to Mayo and Bernays, who sought to weaponize Freudian theory across the workplace, advertising, culture, business and statecraft—indeed, as we argue, in every locus of modern life—this colonization continued via the generation of post-1968 nonconformists that arose from the backlash against Freudian psychoanalysis; the children of the counterculture would not preside over a diminishing of Freudian theory within contemporary life, but an even greater dissemination of its ideas.

This introduction opened with a quotation from *The Interpretation of Dreams* wherein Freud employs an economic metaphor to explain the operation of the unconscious in the production of dreams, and in the sections that followed we have provided a brief historical overview of how Freudian psychoanalysis contributed to the inculcation of what Samo Tomšič terms the 'capitalist unconscious'; that is, the 'intertwining of unconscious satisfaction with the structure and the logic of the capitalist mode of production'.[61] In his reading of the century, Alain Badiou addresses the enigma of the twentieth century as one that ends catastrophically, though it 'kicks off in an exceptional fashion'.[62] Badiou celebrates Freud among a host of figures whose work in literature, science, music and politics energized the early decades of the century; from Einstein's special relativity, to Lenin's October Revolution, to James Joyce's rewriting of the novel, its history is marked by an experimentalism that coincided with some of the great discoveries of modernity. As we have shown, the revolutionary hope that psychoanalysis would free humankind from the repressive injunctions that lead to the onset of neuroses, dissipated as the century progressed. Badiou marks the historical arc of the twentieth century as moving from an initial political project of creating the 'new man' to the eventual waning of the political in the takeover of technology and market capital. 'Ultimately, and right to its very end', he concludes, 'the century will indeed have been the century of the emergence of another humanity, of a radical transformation of what man is'.[63] Stalin's gulags stand as gravestones to the failure of communism, and in lieu of grand ideological alternatives we are living in an age of remarkable advancement in health, medicine, technology, culture and communication. Global capitalism has transformed the lives of individuals as no other socio-economic system in history has done, and populations who still reside beyond the reach of it today are involved in violent struggle to gain access to a system that has inequality hardwired into its structural makeup. In the chapters that follow we consider how the radical transformation of the human has continued in the early decades of the twenty-first century, reading its symptoms under the sign of the late Freud.

Notes

1. Sigmund Freud, *The Interpretation of Dreams*, in *The Standard Edition of the Complete Psychological Works of Sigmund Freud*, trans. by James Strachey, Vol. V (London: Hogarth Press, 1953 [1900]), p. 561.
2. Sigmund Freud, 'On Beginning the Treatment: Further Recommendations on the Technique of Psycho-Analysis I', in *The Standard Edition of the Complete Psychological Works of Sigmund Freud*, trans. by James Strachey, Vol. XII (London: Hogarth Press, 1958 [1913]), pp. 121–44 (131).
3. Freud (1958, p. 132).
4. Eli Zaretsky, *Political Freud: A History* (New York, NY: Columbia University Press, 2015), p. 185.
5. H.J. Eysenck, *Decline and Fall of the Freudian Empire* (Harmondsworth: Penguin Books, 1985), p. 8.
6. See Wendy Brown, *Undoing the Demos: Neoliberalism's Stealth Revolution* (New York, NY: Zone Books, 2015).
7. The chapters that follow focus on the situation of the subject within contemporary neoliberal society in its North American and European dimensions, predominantly centered on examples drawn from the cultural and political landscapes of the United States and United Kingdom.
8. See Joel Whitebook, *Freud: An Intellectual Biography* (New York, NY: Columbia University Press, 2017).
9. See Élisabeth Roudinesco, *Freud: In His Time and Ours*, trans. by Catherine Porter (Cambridge, MA: Harvard University Press, 2016 [2014]).
10. Frederick Crews, *Freud: The Making of an Illusion* (London: Profile Books, 2017), p. 641.
11. Crews (2017, p. 5).
12. Todd Dufresne, *The Late Sigmund Freud: Or, the Last Word on Psychoanalysis, Society and All the Riddles of Life* (Cambridge: Cambridge University Press, 2017), p. 223.
13. Dufresne (2017, p. 67).
14. Todd McGowan, *Capitalism and Desire: The Psychic Cost of Free Markets* (New York, NY: Columbia University Press, 2016), p. 18.
15. Samo Tomšič, *The Capitalist Unconscious: Marx and Lacan* (London: Verso Books, 2015a), p. 3.
16. Ibid.
17. See Tomšič (2015a, p. 99) for a full discussion of dreams, production and Marx's labor theory.

18. Sigmund Freud, *An Autobiographical Study*, in *The Standard Edition of the Complete Psychological Works of Sigmund Freud,* trans. by James Strachey, Vol. XX (London: Hogarth Press, 1959a [1925]), pp. 2–74 (55).
19. For a discussion of the constant pain Freud suffered in later years that resulted from his mouth cancer and the multiple operations he endured, as well as the developing deafness in his right ear, see Peter Gay, *Freud: A Life For Our Time* (Basingstoke: Macmillan Publishers, 1995 [1988]), p. 427.
20. For a more detailed discussion of Freud and the term 'mass' see Céline Surprenant, *Freud's Mass Psychology: Questions of Scale* (Basingstoke: Palgrave Macmillan, 2003).
21. Freud (1959a, p. 59).
22. Sigmund Freud, 'The Claims of Psycho-Analysis to Scientific Interest', in *The Standard Edition of the Complete Psychological Works of Sigmund Freud,* trans. by James Strachey, Vol. XIII (London: Hogarth Press, 1955 [1913]), pp. 163–90 (188).
23. For example, compare the writing of 'The Claims of Psycho-Analysis To Scientific Interest' with Freud's schematizing of the individual within the mass in *An Outline of Psycho-Analysis* for evidence of the more sophisticated approach:

    > We have repeatedly had to insist on the fact that the ego owes its origins as well as the most important of its acquired characteristics to its relation to the real external world. We are thus prepared to assume that the ego's pathological states [...] are founded on a cessation or slackening of that relation to the external world.

    Sigmund Freud, *An Outline of Psycho-Analysis*, in *The Standard Edition of the Complete Psychological Works of Sigmund Freud,* trans. by James Strachey, Vol. XXIII (London: Hogarth Press, 1964a [1940]), pp. 139–207 (201).
24. See Fredric Jameson, *Postmodernism: Or, the Cultural Logic of Late Capitalism* (Durham, NC: Duke University Press, 1991).
25. David Harvey, *A Brief History of Neoliberalism* (Oxford and New York, NY: Oxford University Press, 2005).
26. Brown (2015, pp. 21–2).
27. Brown (2015, p. 122).
28. Brown (2015, p. 10).
29. Ibid.
30. Sigmund Freud, *Civilization and Its Discontents*, in *The Standard Edition of the Complete Psychological Works of Sigmund Freud*, trans. by James Strachey, Vol. XXI (London: Hogarth Press, 1964b [1930]), pp. 59–145 (141).
31. Zaretsky (2015, p. 2).

32. See, for example, Lawrence R. Samuel, *Freud on Madison Avenue: Motivation Research and Subliminal Advertising in America* (Philadelphia, PA: University of Pennsylvania Press, 2010) and Adam Curtis, *The Century of The Self* (BBC Worldwide, 2002).
33. Edward Bernays, *Propaganda* (New York, NY: Ig Publishing, 2005 [1928]), p. 75.
34. Bernays (1928, pp. 75–6).
35. Zaretsky (2015, p. 28).
36. Elton Mayo, *The Human Problems of an Industrial Civilization* (Cambridge, MA: The Murray Printing Company, 1933), p. 127.
37. Ibid.
38. Mayo (1933, p. 159).
39. Mayo (1933, p. 54).
40. Mayo (1933, p. 93).
41. Mayo (1933, p. 177).
42. Mayo (1933, p. 171).
43. Wilhelm Reich, *The Mass Psychology of Fascism*, trans. by Mary Boyd Higgins (New York, NY: Farrar, Straus and Giroux, 1970 [1933]), p. 18.
44. Reich (1970, p. 19).
45. Reich (1970, p. 27).
46. Reich (1970, p. 27).
47. Reich (1970, p. 30).
48. Sigmund Freud, *The Question of Lay Analysis: Conversations with an Impartial Person*, in *The Standard Edition of the Complete Psychological Works of Sigmund Freud*, trans. by James Strachey, Vol. XX (London: Hogarth Press, 1959b [1926]), pp. 177–258 (236).
49. See Gilles Deleuze and Félix Guattari, *Anti-Oedipus: Capitalism and Schizophrenia*, trans. by Robert Hurley, Mark Seem, and Helen R. Lane (London: Continuum, 2004a [1972]), p. 31.
50. Deleuze and Guattari (2004a, p. 31).
51. Deleuze and Guattari (2004a, p. 31).
52. Reich (1970, p. 30).
53. Ibid.
54. R.D. Laing, *The Politics of Experience and The Bird of Paradise* (New York, NY: Pantheon Books, 1967), p. 4.
55. Interview with Arthur Miller in Adam Curtis, *The Century of the Self* (BBC Worldwide, 2002).
56. Bernays (1928, p. 37).
57. V.I. Lenin, 'The Second Congress of the Communist International', from the *Collected Works*, trans. by Julius Katzer, 4th Ed. Vol. III (Moscow: Progress Publishers, 1965), p. 215.

58. Luc Boltanski and Eve Chiapello, *The New Spirit of Capitalism*, trans. by Gregory Elliott (London: Verso, 2004 [1999]), p. 27.
59. Boltanski and Chiapello (2004, p. 436).
60. Boltanski and Chiapello (2004, p. 97).
61. Tomšič (2015a, pp. 108–9).
62. Alain Badiou, *The Century*, trans. by Alberto Toscano (Cambridge and Malden, MA: Polity, 2007 [2005]), p. 6.
63. Badiou (2007, p. 10).

Works Cited

Alain Badiou, *The Century*, trans. by Alberto Toscano (Cambridge and Malden, MA: Polity, 2007 [2005]).

Wendy Brown, *Undoing the Demos: Neoliberalism's Stealth Revolution* (New York, NY: Zone Books, 2015).

Edward Bernays, *Propaganda* (New York, NY: Ig Publishing, 2005 [1928]).

Luc Boltanski and Eve Chiapello, *The New Spirit of Capitalism*, trans. by Gregory Elliott (London: Verso, 2004 [1999]).

Frederick Crews, *Freud: The Making of an Illusion* (London: Profile Books, 2017).

Gilles Deleuze and Félix Guattari, *Anti-Oedipus: Capitalism and Schizophrenia*, trans. by Robert Hurley, Mark Seem, and Helen R. Lane (London: Continuum, 2004 [1972]).

Todd Dufresne, *The Late Sigmund Freud: Or, the Last Word on Psychoanalysis, Society and All the Riddles of Life* (Cambridge: Cambridge University Press, 2017).

H.J. Eysenck, *Decline and Fall of the Freudian Empire* (Harmondsworth: Penguin Books, 1985).

Peter Gay, *Freud: A Life For Our Time* (Basingstoke: Macmillan Publishers, 1995 [1988]).

Sigmund Freud, *The Interpretation of Dreams*, in *The Standard Edition of the Complete Psychological Works of Sigmund Freud*, trans. by James Strachey, Vol. V (London: Hogarth Press, 1953 [1900]).

Sigmund Freud, 'The Claims of Psycho-Analysis to Scientific Interest', in *The Standard Edition of the Complete Psychological Works of Sigmund Freud*, trans. by James Strachey, Vol. XIII (London: Hogarth Press, 1955 [1913]).

Sigmund Freud, 'On Beginning the Treatment: Further Recommendations on the Technique of Psycho-Analysis I', in *The Standard Edition of the Complete Psychological Works of Sigmund Freud*, trans. by James Strachey, Vol. XII (London: Hogarth Press, 1958 [1913]).

Sigmund Freud, *An Autobiographical Study*, in *The Standard Edition of the Complete Psychological Works of Sigmund Freud*, trans. by James Strachey, Vol. XX (London: Hogarth Press, 1959 [1925]).

Sigmund Freud, *The Question of Lay Analysis: Conversations with an Impartial Person*, in *The Standard Edition of the Complete Psychological Works of Sigmund Freud*, trans. by James Strachey, Vol. XX (London: Hogarth Press, 1959 [1926]).

Sigmund Freud, *Civilization and Its Discontents*, in *The Standard Edition of the Complete Psychological Works of Sigmund Freud*, trans. by James Strachey, Vol. XXI (London: Hogarth Press, 1964 [1930]).

Sigmund Freud, *An Outline of Psycho-Analysis*, in *The Standard Edition of the Complete Psychological Works of Sigmund Freud*, trans. by James Strachey, Vol. XXIII (London: Hogarth Press, 1964 [1940]).

David Harvey, *A Brief History of Neoliberalism* (Oxford and New York, NY: Oxford University Press, 2005).

Fredric Jameson, *Postmodernism: Or, the Cultural Logic of Late Capitalism* (Durham, NC: Duke University Press, 1991).

R.D. Laing, *The Politics of Experience and The Bird of Paradise* (New York, NY: Pantheon Books, 1967).

V.I. Lenin, 'The Second Congress of the Communist International', from the *Collected Works*, trans. by Julius Katzer, 4th Ed. Vol. III (Moscow: Progress Publishers, 1965).

Elton Mayo, *The Human Problems of an Industrial Civilization* (Cambridge, MA: The Murray Printing Company, 1933).

Todd McGowan, *Capitalism and Desire: The Psychic Cost of Free Markets* (New York, NY: Columbia University Press, 2016).

Wilhelm Reich, *The Mass Psychology of Fascism*, trans. by Mary Boyd Higgins (New York, NY: Farrar, Straus and Giroux, 1970 [1933]).

Élisabeth Roudinesco, *Freud: In His Time and Ours*, trans. by Catherine Porter (Cambridge, MA: Harvard University Press, 2016 [2014]).

Céline Surprenant, *Freud's Mass Psychology: Questions of Scale* (Basingstoke: Palgrave Macmillan, 2003).

Samo Tomšič, *The Capitalist Unconscious: Marx and Lacan* (London: Verso Books, 2015).

Joel Whitebook, *Freud: An Intellectual Biography* (New York, NY: Columbia University Press, 2017).

Eli Zaretsky, *Political Freud: A History* (New York, NY: Columbia University Press, 2015).

CHAPTER 2

A Politics of Freud

The Elite: 'The Dictatorship of Reason'

With the creation of its own political body, the International Psychoanalytical Association (IPA), psychoanalysis has since its inception cultivated an internal politics and division, leading ultimately to a schism between its conservative orthodox and radical wings; more curiously still, the politics at work in its internal factions (dynastic leadership, faithful disciples and renegade tyros included) has been consistently disavowed from the project of psychoanalysis itself in order to maintain the principle of scientific rationality to which it aspires.[1] In his essay 'Freud and the Political' (2008) Mladen Dolar has argued that, despite Freud's protestations, psychoanalysis has always been political. Dolar characterizes the work undertaken by Freud later in his life as a turn to the social, yet proposes that, although the diagnostic eye of the late Freud moves towards society and the human condition, there remains in the key words recurring throughout his work of this period an ambivalence that evidences a reluctance for psychoanalysis to be read as overtly political. Observing an elusiveness in what he categorizes as his 'social writings', Dolar demonstrates that the terms employed by Freud minimize their political valence: instead of population, we have 'group' or 'mass'; instead of state, Freud adopts the term 'civilization'; and instead of society, he mobilizes 'culture'.[2] Dolar interprets these linguistic choices as a means to ensure that psychoanalysis remains focused on the individual within society, arguing that Freud's preferred

M.-D. Dick, R. McLaughlan, *Late Capitalist Freud in Literary, Cultural, and Political Theory*,
https://doi.org/10.1007/978-3-030-47194-1_2

terminology functions to 'depoliticize' psychoanalysis.[3] In what sense, then, can we consider psychoanalysis as political either in its own historiography or as a discourse for theorizing the social?.

In the first section of this chapter we trace the political turn in two late texts of Freud, reading *The Future of an Illusion* and *Why War?* as representative of Freud's theoretical move away from the clinic and towards society. Deploying primary texts alongside contemporary political and psychoanalytical theory, we outline Freud's argument for social organization centered around the creation of an 'elite' and consider how this proposal presages current political scenes. We examine the social, cultural and ideological afterlife of the late Freud's political turn, characterized by a developing pessimism regarding human nature and his advocating for the establishment of a secular 'dictatorship of reason', to propose that a genealogical strand of our contemporary elite can be traced back through the middle classes, where it emerged as a dominant form of social organization in the twentieth century, to Freud's political vision. Our second section considers Freud's application of individual psychology to the social order and how the theories conceptualized within this social turn might be mobilized to analyze the phenomenon of contemporary political populism. Using Donald Trump's locker room defense as our case study, we turn again to the late Freudian writings to demonstrate that, though he may have advocated for the creation of a secular elite to manage the unconscious desires and wishes of citizens, at the historical juncture within which Freud was writing his theory was unable to predict how contemporary leaders would utilize the ideas outlined in *Group Psychology and the Analysis of the Ego* to lead a revolt against his 'dictatorship of reason'. Freud's suspicion of the masses is not unique, being situated within a wider context of Hobbesian social theory and evidenced in interwar and post-war skepticism of the potential and limits of mass democracy. Renewals of Freudian psychoanalysis, such as Joel Whitebook's *Perversion and Utopia* (1995), have confirmed through readings of contemporary political events the first-generation Frankfurt School belief in the paradox of mass democracy, the threat posed by Enlightenment rationality and the ongoing risk to late twentieth century society of totalitarian leaders.[4] In this chapter we continue in the tradition of this analysis but attend to specific historical mechanisms which suggest that the current political situation of the Euro-American axis, including the rise of populism and implications of the later neoliberal model for post-millennial formations of political rationality, affords particular illumination of the Freudian position.

While Friedrich Nietzsche has been implicated in the rise of totalitarian thinking and Marx stands accused of leading to the gulags, history has failed to fully indict Freud for the intellectual influence his late work has had upon the organizational structuration of the neoliberal century. The anti-psychiatry movement of the twentieth century concentrated on psychoanalysis as a repressive system, but remained silent on the late writing of Freud and its explicit turn towards an interest in the political. Part prescription, part prophesy, his vision of a wealth-creating state—wherein the lazy masses are disciplined by a rational class schooled in psychodynamics—stands surprisingly under-accused. In the lecture on *Weltanschauung* taken from *New Introductory Lectures on Psycho-Analysis*, Freud stresses that psychoanalysis should not be perceived as a 'world-view' [*Weltanschauung*]: '[p]sycho-analysis, in my opinion, is incapable of creating a *Weltanschauung* of its own. It does not need one; it is a part of science and can adhere to the scientific *Weltanschauung*'.[5] Not for the first time, Freud presents the reader with a contradictory statement that belies his desired intention for psychoanalysis. His disavowal of psychoanalysis as the dissemination of a political *Weltanschauung* can, by way of a generous interpretation, be justified on the basis that Freud did not live long enough to witness the transformation of his work into ideology. Yet Freud's insistence that psychoanalysis comprises another branch of a larger scientific *Weltanschauung* is consistent with a persistent anxiety that nagged him throughout his career: that psychoanalysis would be regarded as illegitimate, a pseudo-science. For Freud, who positioned himself within an intellectual genealogy preceded by Darwin and Copernicus, science was the Enlightenment triumph of empiricism over religious mysticism. Part of the ire that fired his attacks on Jung concerned the latter's attempt to shift psychoanalysis in the direction of the numinous as against Freud's association of religion with unreason. Although occasionally unconventional in its methodological approach, Freud yearned for psychoanalysis to be considered among a scientific constellation that included physics, biology, chemistry, medicine and neurology. He considered that the pioneering discoveries made in the field of psychology—the talking cure, the instinctual life of subjects, the existence of the unconscious—qualified psychoanalysis as a science predicated upon reason.

Two late texts from the Freudian canon embody this coupling of an absolute faith in reason with a dismissal of religion as nothing more than an elaborate Oedipal production, combining them towards an increasingly pessimistic understanding of humanity. Both *The Future of an Illusion* and

Why War? also represent textual shifts from the realm of the clinical into that of the political, as Freud's focus moves from the individual to the social. *The Future of an Illusion* elucidates Freud's conviction that religious belief represents a form of wish fulfilment. As the title of the book indicates, Freud conceives of religion as an artifice arising from an infantile experience of helplessness negotiated by the construction of a fantasy paternal figure in possession of an all-powerful aura, with the fantasy then reworked in the creation of a God who allays feelings of vulnerability and isolation. The text continues today to be read alongside Freud's other treaties on the psychic origins of religious faith, such as *Moses and Monotheism* (1939), yet from its opening chapter, Freud advances a proposition of the structures he considers necessary to implement in order to be able to control the masses. The significance of this book lies not only in its existence as a rejoinder to the claim, inaugurated and propagated by Freud himself, that psychoanalysis does not provide a *Weltanschauung* beyond the scientific: in its discussion of mass psychology and social structuration it also constitutes a blueprint for the political organization of late capitalism and anticipates its organization.

The first chapter of *The Future of an Illusion* constitutes a rehearsal of some of the claims that Freud will later develop in *Civilization and Its Discontents*; pressed for space and eager to begin his analysis of religion as an Oedipal illusion, Freud's prose is terse and his points sharp. Not yet at the stage where he is able to provide a sustained explanation for man's inherent aggression, Freud instead makes a series of arresting statements that express his enveloping cynicism. Drawing upon the title of Henrik Ibsen's play *An Enemy of the People* (1882), he declares that 'every individual is virtually an enemy of civilization', presenting a bleak vision of a humanity composed of violent beings who struggle to control the desires that govern their psyches.[6] Freud extends his psychoanalytic schematizing of humankind in the direction of the socio-anthropological when he observes that 'little as men are able to exist in isolation', they are not necessarily willing to make the 'sacrifices which civilization expects of them in order to make a communal life possible'.[7] The first chapter of *The Future of an Illusion* contains an oblique rejection of communism, with Freud endorsing the psychosocial principles of capitalism:

> It seems rather that every civilization must be built up on coercion and renunciation of instinct; it does not even seem certain that if coercion were

> to cease the majority of human beings would be prepared to undertake to perform the work necessary for acquiring new wealth.[8]

If citizens are the 'enemy of civilization', that is to say irrational subjects governed by selfish self-interest, or the very portrait of unreason, then Freud's remedy is to return to an Enlightenment secularism that privileges empiricism and reason above all else: '[t]hus civilization has to be defended against the individual, and its regulations, institutions and commands are directed to that task'.[9]

Freud's interest in the individual is inherently related to the wellbeing of society, defined in relation to its capital creation. This configuration of individuals as 'destructive' requires the implementation of mechanisms of control that will inoculate 'anti-social' impulses in order to facilitate 'new wealth' production. In *Civilization and Its Discontents*, Freud claims never to have seriously engaged with Marxist theory; yet, the opening sections of *The Future of an Illusion* read like a love letter to capitalist democracy, wherein regulatory control at the level of the state should be engineered towards the production of capital. Although Freud insisted that there was no end goal to analysis, this caveat failed to pacify critics who suspected that psychoanalysis was involved in a campaign to rehabilitate certain individuals, once deemed to be a form of social surplus, back into the labor market for the benefit of the greater social good. Certainly, *The Future of an Illusion* finds Freud at his most evangelical in espousing the tenets that would define bourgeois monopoly capitalism, the success of which depended upon the successful regulation of subjects' libidinal and aggressive tendencies. Individuals require demonstrative coercion from the state to encourage them to renounce their instincts for selfishness and destruction in order for wealth to be produced. This public dimension is crucial for Freud because without a constant reminder that the needs of society be privileged over individual needs, individuals will prioritize their own narcissistic pleasures.

Freud's next conceptual step in the treatise is to visualize an architecture of power that can be implemented to facilitate the coercion of individuals in the pursuit of social regulation. It is in this diagnosis and prescription that we can retrospectively detect a social manifesto in embryonic form, one that will eventually find analogy with Foucault's disciplinary society in the following decades:

> It is just as impossible to do without control of the mass by a minority as it is to dispense with coercion in the work of civilization. For masses are lazy and unintelligent; they have no love for instinctual renunciation, and they are not to be convinced by argument of its inevitability; and the individuals composing them support one another in giving free rein to their indiscipline. It is only through the influence of individuals who can set an example and whom masses recognize as their leaders that they can be induced to perform the work and undergo the renunciations on which the existence of civilization depends.[10]

Freud here argues for the installation of an elite to act as role models in the renunciation of their desires at the very highest echelons of society. If subjects are enemies of civilization who need to be coerced in giving up their libidinal pleasures in the interest of the socius, it follows that any qualified candidate must have an ego of considerable strength to be able to check the demands of their own unconscious and that narcissists, who are vulnerable to the intoxicating effects of power, need not apply. Throughout *The Future of an Illusion*, Freud returns to the relationship between organized religion and education, characterizing the former as a necessary phase in the developmental history of civilization and transposing his theories of psychosexual development on to the history of humankind. As psychoanalysis teaches us that in order to progress towards adulthood, individuals must navigate a period of neurosis—with those unable to do so on their own requiring the help of an analyst—Freud retools that psychosexual model of individual development to explain the evolutionary origins of religion in the history of civilization-making. Religion is consequently reworked as 'the universal obsessional neurosis of humanity' that, similar to the obsessional neurosis of children, originates 'out of the Oedipus complex, out of the relation to the father'.[11] In order for civilization to progress beyond this epochal moment of obsessional neurosis there needs to be a 'turning-away from religion' and, as for the obsessional neurotics who stepped into Freud's world of *Berggasse 19* seeking the aid of the analyst-guide, resolution can be accomplished only under the guidance of a 'race of men who have renounced all illusions'.[12] Echoes of Marx can be found in Freud's belief that a cadre of enlightenment agents, schooled in scientific reason and presumably having undergone an analysis, will effect the overthrow of religious authority in Europe. Mirroring Marx's notion of the sections of the bourgeoisie who will splinter off to form the intellectual wing of the proletariat, these rational beings would undertake the task of uncoupling religion from education and in doing so free the masses from the illusory sway of religious mythology. Achieving Freudian consciousness is no easy task; religion is transformed from an opiate to a sort of Oedipal Ambien for the masses: '[a] man who has been taking sleeping draughts for tens of years is naturally unable to sleep if his sleeping draught is taken away from him'.[13] This new wing comprised of figures of superego authority would ultimately be responsible for the establishment of the organizational apparatuses that would manage civilization in a post-religious world; they must be perfect Freudian creations, or the social order risks disintegration:

> All is well if these leaders are persons who possess superior insight into the necessities of life and who have risen to the height of mastering their own instinctual wishes. But there is a danger that in order not to lose their influence they may give way to the mass more than it gives way to them, and it therefore seems necessary that they shall be independent of the mass by having means to power at their disposal.[14]

In *The Future of an Illusion* Freud advocates for the creation of a secular dictatorship governed by reason as its logos. Democracy is an imperfect system, as it indulges the capricious nature of citizens and produces results through elections that are detrimental to society. A dictatorship of Freudian beings could be trusted to govern not in their own self-interest but for the good of everyone, and Freud's belief in the inherent social good that accompanies wealth creation provides the ethical alibi that allows him essentially to argue at this stage for the organized repression of libidinal desire at the level of the state.[15]

When invited by Albert Einstein to correspond on the topic of war, Freud understood the powerful opportunity that the request to converse with the most famous scientist since Darwin presented for his tireless pursuit to confirm psychoanalysis as scientifically legitimate. After their correspondence had been published in 1933 under the title of *Warum Krieg?* (*Why War?*), Freud quickly dispatched a copy to the Italian fascist leader Benito Mussolini, scribbling the following inscription in the book: '[t]o Benito Mussolini, from an old man who greets in the ruler, the *Hero of Culture*'.[16] The relationship between psychoanalysis and European fascism is a particularly complicated one, made all the more so when Jung's engagement with National Socialism is factored into the equation, but Freud was more guarded in his interactions with political leaders. In a prefatory note to the publication of *Moses and Monotheism* Freud displays a pragmatic relativism when describing the historical moment during which he is writing as a 'remarkable period', submitting that profound social advancement had been realized in Europe though at the cost of human liberty.[17] Freud understood that the Stalinist experiment propelled Russia into an age of secular modernity, the people of the Soviet Union living free of the '"opium" of religion' and with 'a reasonable amount of sexual liberty'; yet such Freudian ideals had been realized by way of 'the most cruel coercion' that had removed 'any possibility of freedom of thought'.[18] Freud's political writings exhibit a lasting fascination with the problem of how to maintain order in an age of increasing human aggression, as exemplified in the extension of his pragmatic evaluation of Stalin's socialism to Mussolini's fascistic training of the Italian people through violence into a population that valued 'orderliness and a sense of duty', while also remaining critical of the totalitarian force that had facilitated such rapid social transformations.[19] Although he possessed an appreciation for glamorous figures synonymous with conquest—Hannibal and Napoleon among the examples—Freud was wary of dictators. Nevertheless, *Why War?* advances a curious solution to the problem posed by the lazy and unintelligent masses, with their in-built proclivity to aggression:

> One instance of the innate and ineradicable inequality of men is their tendency to fall into the two classes of leaders and followers. The latter constitute the vast majority; they stand in need of an authority which will make decisions for them and to which they for the most part offer an unqualified submission. This suggests that more care should be taken than hitherto to educate an upper stratum of men with independent minds, not open to intimidation and eager in the pursuit of truth, whose business it would be to give direction to the dependent masses.[20]

This 'upper stratum of men' that would break off from the masses to form a ruling elite in the interests of safeguarding civilization from the libidinal instinct of the general population recalls the earlier proposal made in *The Future of an Illusion*. Freud again insists that educated elites should be established within the centers of government to regulate the everyday unconscious lives of citizens and, true to his secularist convictions, states that they will be defined by the possession of a strength of will to discipline desire to reason: '[t]he ideal condition of things would of course be a community of men who had subordinated their instinctual life to the dictatorship of reason. [...] But in all probability that is a Utopian expectation'.[21] As already demonstrated by the history of the French Revolution in the eighteenth century, the organization of society according to secular rationalism could have bloody ends. Freud's caveat that the realization of his vision would remain a dream anticipates the way in which grand utopian concepts of the nineteenth century were implemented to devastating effect in the twentieth, and presumes a quiet admission that the ideal psychoanalytic subject, for whom all unconscious desires can be brought into check, is, in fact, an impossible one. Freud's unconvincing engagement with Marxist political philosophy is rendered irrelevant when considered alongside *The Future of an Illusion* and *Why War?* (not to mention *Beyond The Pleasure Principle* and *Civilization and Its Discontents*), for what he ultimately argues in this later work is that all political utopian visions remain provisional. What undermines utopia, from a psychoanalytic perspective, are the individuals that inhabit them.

Freud's late work is watermarked by the fact that it views early twentieth-century civilization as staggering on the cusp of chaos. This reversal of a Marxist teleology envisages society as progressing at the same time as humanity regresses towards a more primitive order of being, one that would be defined by unchecked aggression—be it psychological, physical or sexual—enacted upon other subjects with sheer abandon, were social domination not to be imposed to confine it. For all that Freud's pragmatism relating to a societal need for mass control appears to confirm his own increasingly misanthropic outlook, a more positive reading might still be recovered. The fact that communal living is made possible by the social contract that exists to curb instinctual drives and what is more, that some communities thrive and evolve, is nothing short of a miracle when humanity is approached through the lens of the late Freud. Despite such an attempt to read a latent positivity in the pages of the later work, and although such a strain undoubtedly exists to be found, Freud's cynicism in the face of utopian dreaming is defined by a belief that began to take hold within him towards the end of his life, that of the famous '*homo homini lupus*'.[22]

The intellectual afterlife of Freud's desire for the inauguration of a 'dictatorship of reason' continues to give shape to our contemporary moment. In *Undoing the Demos: Neoliberalism's Stealth Revolution* (2015), Wendy Brown sets forth a critique of neoliberalism that takes as its departure Foucault's rethinking of *homo oeconomicus* as the 'entrepreneurial self', tracing a history of the concept of neoliberalism as it has gone beyond economic theory to pervade and structure an economized democracy generated in the ideology of the market, thus providing a model of political rationality that encompasses every sphere of life.[23] A reading of late Freud adds a psychoanalytic dimension to the political theory of late capitalism, providing insight into an earlier twentieth-century formulation even as it also supports Brown's careful summarizing of the earlier origins of neoliberalism. Though Brown, following Foucault, dates its origins to the mid-century, *The Future of an Illusion* might be considered a premonition of the movement from the ordering of society through capitalism as a financial system to late capitalist total economization. Explaining the importance of psychology to the governance of modern civilization, Freud foresees that 'the emphasis has moved over from the material to the mental', presaging the grounds of neoliberalism's success in occupying our subjectivity by disarticulating from its (im)material substrate, finance capital, to operate through mental colonization and reproduction.[24] Freud's short work reads in parts like a dream of Friedrich Hayek and Milton Friedman, a blueprint for neoliberal reason as a corrective to a morbid socius, and one that would produce future generations of productive citizens. In it, Freud aspires to an auto-disciplined society wherein cultural regulation functions to produce a generation whose belief in reason engenders a new attitude to society:

> They will feel it as a possession of their very own and will be ready for its sake to make the sacrifices as regards work and instinctual satisfaction that are necessary for its preservation. They will be able to do without coercion and will differ little from their leaders. If no culture has so far produced human masses of such a quality, it is because no culture has yet devised regulations which will influence men in this way, and in particular from childhood onwards.[25]

What is elsewhere in the treatise referred to as a process of internalized coercion creates a productive social being whose descendants are the entrepreneurial self of Foucault, and the economized self of Wendy Brown. In this, Freud's 'dictatorship of reason' finds its perfect expression in neoliberal rationality, a form of cultural regulation promoted by an elite composed of rulers both elected and unelected, who purport to close the affective gap between the leader of culture and the demos even as it becomes financially the largest in history, but is also reproduced by the masses, or democratic body.

Freud also goes some way to rationalizing the feelings of the 99% when he alludes to the expectation that the 'underprivileged classes will envy the favoured ones their privileges', inferring that from this iniquity arise the conditions either for liberation or revolt.[26] In so far as neoliberal reason has colonized and been internalized by the contemporary social psyche, the possibility of revolution against the upper stratum is now questionable. As the contemporary 'dictatorship of reason', neoliberal rationality transforms subjects into a mass human capital such that Freud's ostensible prohibition becomes an uncanny prevision. *The Future of an Illusion* stages our political scene in its diagnosis of the interaction between the cultural unit and the 'cultural ideal' or shared capital by which the value of a civilization is measured.[27] Through the 'narcissistic satisfaction' afforded by the shared ideal that suppresses tension arising from iniquity within the cultural unit, the mass learns to identify with the minority ruling class.[28] Moreover, those who belong to the suppressed class obtain a further indirect satisfaction that prevents them from acting in their own interests through becoming 'emotionally attached to their masters', so that 'they may see in them their ideals'.[29] This reflective relation, premised on a cultural superstructure that develops from the governing ideology of the ruling minority, not only quietens but actively co-opts the masses to their own oppression.

In *Analysis Terminable and Interminable*, Freud discusses the efficacy of psychoanalytic practice in enacting a permanent resolution to the symptomology of neurotics. Wearied by having had to flee from the Nazis to London and pained by the oral cancer that would result in his having to wear a prosthesis to separate his mouth and nasal cavity, Freud's fatigue extends to the redemptive value of psychoanalysis. Referring to it as 'the third of those "impossible" professions which one can be sure beforehand of achieving unsatisfying results'—the other two being education and government—Freud considers whether the talking cure had any claim to be a cure at all.[30] Warning against psychoanalysis's ability to offer prophylactic protection to neurotic patients once they had left the clinician's room, Freud cautions his followers that it cannot vaccinate against future instinctual conflicts and discourages an inflated confidence in analysis to bring about a successful resolution in the lives of patients. While not necessarily an 'endless business', the clinical practitioners of Freud's theories must guard against the 'exaggerated expectations' of patients.[31] Yet for all the uncertainty that pervades *Analysis Terminable and Interminable*, Freud does maintain a conviction in psychoanalysis's ability to ensure social stability even if it is ultimately impossible to attain 'a level of absolute psychical normality'.[32]

In 1944 at Bretton Woods, seven hundred and thirty-two delegates from forty-four allied nations met to institute a dictatorship of post-war reason that would pave the way to neoliberalism, first along the mid-century free-market model and then in its increasingly pervasive late twentieth-century and contemporary manifestations. The emergence in the post-war era of supranational peacekeeping institutions (the United Nations and European Economic Community, later the European Union) installed the tiers of unelected technocrats to maintain the burgeoning global bureaucracy that would support it. With the collapse of the Berlin Wall in 1989 and the alleged demise of grand narratives of ideological thinking, politicians in the West began to implement the sort of Freudian managerialism pioneered earlier in the century by Elton Mayo. Nation states were to be run like corporations, with stability the primary political message of Western political life. In the days after the financial crash of 2008, the EU under the control of the European Central Bank implemented austerity as a means to chastise against profligacy, and the mantra of 'balancing the books' became the clarion call of Jean-Claude Trichet and Wolfgang Schäuble.[33] To the general populace, who not only had played no part in the crash but had dutifully abided by market logic, this brand of retrospective superego legislation after a period of death drive economics—after all deregulation, to paraphrase Gordon Brown, was to bring an end to boom and bust economics—was considered to be grossly unfair. Why should the many have to pay for the mistakes of the few?. It has since transpired that the recession signaled an important point in time in the intellectual history of Freud's upper stratum of psychoanalytic social scientists, in that it doubled as the moment when a global public started to lose trust in the paternalistic managerialism that shaped their lives at both national and global levels. The turn towards a politics of 'commonsense' was summed up by then-Justice Secretary Michael Gove's pronouncement that people in Britain 'have had enough of experts'.[34] Harnessing Brexiteer distrust of shadow empires, Gove assumed a populist stance premised on asserting a reversion to the reasoned opinion of the majority when he stated that 'I'm not asking the public to trust me. I'm asking them to trust themselves'.[35] Whether taking back control or draining the swamp, both Brexit and Trump deal a blow to Freud's 'dictatorship of reason' as examples of populist movements in a post-truth world.

'Locker Room Talk'

In a 2005 recording obtained by *The Washington Post*, the reality TV star and future President of the United States, Donald Trump, was captured on tape while in conversation with Billy Bush for *Access Hollywood*. Trump and Bush were discussing the actress Arianne Zucker:

Trump: Yeah, that's her. With the gold. I better use some Tic Tacs just in case I start kissing her. You know, I'm automatically attracted to beautiful—I just start kissing them. It's like a magnet. Just kiss. I don't even wait. And when you're a star, they let you do it. You can do anything.
Bush: Whatever you want.
Trump: Grab 'em by the pussy. You can do anything.[36]

The general political consensus of the Washington commentariat was that this tape would end Trump's hopes of becoming the forty-fifth President of the United States. Yet for all the shock and revulsion vented in the aftermath of the leaked conversation, Trump's tilt at the presidency did not come undone and, indeed, continued unaffected. In fact, this was a pivotal moment in the global political narrative of the Trump era, which has increasingly become defined as a stability paradoxically engendered by constant chaos: daily, sometimes hourly, scandals, that in a different climate would each on their own sink a leader, barely register in the white noise of the 24/7 news cycle. When confronted with the capriciousness, lascivious behavior, sexual immaturity or petulance of Trump (read any tweet of his on any day), shock, including that of impeachment, fails to register in the way it used to: cultural commentators react with incredulity, late night talk show hosts lampoon in monologues and various activist groups react with anger, but these voices now seem like the old echoes of a previous world order.

Trump's sexual *braggadocio* and Bush's titillation stage an adolescent scene, the crude talk that passed between the two men on the bus functioning as a form of discursive play whereby homosocial bonds are strengthened via a sexual desire for the female other. Of course, psychoanalysis makes a great deal out of such forms of play; we only need to think back to the *fort/da* of Freud's grandson Ernst to understand that the games we play are never frivolous, but avenues to redirect impulses deemed too shameful by the ego to be allowed conscious articulation. Yet it was in his defense of this exchange that Trump displayed a savvy understanding of desire as a powerful psychic force and also of how his manipulation of a collective desire would eventually result in his election to the White House. During the second Presidential debate with Hillary Clinton, held in October 2016, Trump offered three iterations of the same defense:

> I don't think you understood what was—this was locker room talk. I'm not proud of it. I apologize to my family. I apologize to the American people. Certainly I'm not proud of it. But this is locker room talk.[37]

Later in the debate, Trump reiterates the same analogy by way of apology:

> Yes, I'm very embarrassed by it. I hate it. But it's locker room talk, and it's one of those things. I will knock the hell out of ISIS. We're going to defeat ISIS. ISIS happened a number of years ago in a vacuum that was left because of bad judgment. And I will tell you, I will take care of ISIS.[38]

Deflecting sexual harassment via militaristic libido, Trump maintained the defense introduced in the original statement released two days prior and immediately following the leaking of the video:

> This was locker-room banter, a private conversation that took place many years ago. Bill Clinton has said far worse to me on the golf course—not even close. I apologize if anyone was offended.[39]

At the time of writing and with a new election campaign underway, the faux-contrite tone of the exculpation itself seems distant in a Presidency now defined by a refusal to acknowledge private impropriety once made public, but the interaction remains signal for the way in which Trump would begin to construct the dialectic between the private and public, silent and spoken. The two-pronged defense relies at the same time on a claiming and disavowing of desire, careful to appeal to his presumed constituency while at the same time paying lip service to contemporary PR optics. The interpellation of Clinton not only establishes Trump's credentials for leadership and situates them within an American genealogy of charismatic sexual aggressors in office, but also insinuates a shared history, gesturing simultaneously to how apparent political oppositions are united by a belief in free-market economic policies. The reference to the golf course subtly diminishes apparent differences between the two and, more importantly still, extends the locker room analogy to another fraternal social space. The comments meanwhile also tapped into another 2016 election narrative, one that represented Hillary as a dynastic inheritor whose feminist ticket was a veneer for power-appropriation. Trump portrayed himself by contrast as an antidote to the career politician, a Washington outsider whose desires should be compared favorably to those of Bill Clinton—'Mine are words, and his is action'.[40] Depicting a David against the Goliath of two politicos who had schemed in a subversive partnership, he denounced his opponent as complicit in a campaign of abuse.

Trump's presidency to date has been characterized by a dialectical oscillation between the covert and overt.[41] In the metaphor of the locker room, he reveals what is seemingly concealed by reserving it to a sequestered space and figuratively creates such a space for the expression of private views in public discourse. Unlike Richard Nixon—another President whose tenure was marked by secret recording—Trump is not a cunning political Machiavel, yet his use of 'locker room talk' as a defense is predicated upon an intuitive but sophisticated understanding of desire as it operates within group psychology. Contrary to accepted wisdom that such behavior would play badly to an evangelical Republican base—who knew that tax cuts could allay issues of morality? —that Trump continues to enjoy the support of a constituency willing to disregard such sexual indiscretions is further evidence of his unorthodox political status. Trump's sexual promiscuity is understood as indexed to his position as a figure of apparently immense wealth and, now, power, but more interestingly is subtextually linked to the 'common-sense' approach he purports to bring to the Augean stables of Washington, which has an underlying affinity with the common-sense legitimation of neoliberal rationality. As unconventional a President as Trump is, there exists a modern corollary in the figure of the ex-Italian Prime Minister, Silvio Berlusconi. Trump's reality TV status pales when compared to Berlusconi's ownership of Italian media, used to launch a populist political career that was likewise marked by scandal and accusations of corruption. Similarities between the two extend beyond the sexual, as both men have cultivated a public image that relies upon the interplay of provocation and denial. Slavoj Žižek's analysis of Berlusconi in *Living in the End Times* (2010) anticipates the rise of Trumpian presidential behavior: discerning an epochal shift in the ownership of a conservative moralism, Žižek argues that the Right has become 'more and more openly vulgar' and that 'it is perhaps the task [...] of the Left to restore some simple good manners'.[42] Žižek takes exception to the way in which Berlusconi mobilizes the tease for his political gain—'the public display of private obscenities, the indecent confessions on TV shows, the shameless mixture of politics and private business interests, all this gradually creates a dangerous moral vacuum'—and implies that his political survival issues too from an eradication of the boundary between private act and public shame.[43] The trick of Berlusconi, and arguably also of Trump, lies in the way in which his immorality became part of his political self-styling: '[a]s the Marx Brothers might have put it, "this man may look like a corrupt idiot and act like a corrupt idiot, but don't let that deceive you—he *is* a corrupt idiot"'.[44] Understood in this context, Trump's citing of 'locker room talk' not only further complicates the binaries of public/private, overt/covert, but the obvious insincerity of his apology reveals how he intends to mask his duplicitousness by making a spectacle of it.

The insincerity of Trump's locker room defense is important to register for its implication that we are all guilty of locker room talk. In Freudian terms, we are each of us required to repress our libidinal selves in order to co-exist as a society. In social terms, we are comfortable with the idea that people do not always act with consistency; when they behave inconsistently with the dominant mores, they disavow those actions: 'I don't know what came over me'; 'I wasn't acting as myself'; 'it was out of character'. This should be nothing shocking. In fact, reality functions as an extended repressed consciousness: although they cannot admit to it, they know exactly what came over them; it *is* ourselves that we recognize and must therefore distance, for the logic of social cohabitation requires a constant repression of that which we otherwise might wish to say or do. In this sense, the metaphor of the locker room is that of a sanctioned space or structured outlet that admits of those dual levels of discourse: one a sustained, public voice, and the other the breaking-through of that which can otherwise not be voiced within the strictures of society. If we follow this Freudian logic, it is notable that in a contemporary age that advocates for the right of expression of our 'authentic' selves, those who consider themselves liberal democrats can create a public imago projecting 'authenticity' to conceal such desires of the subject; in these terms, 'authenticity' is in fact derived from a set of ostensibly democratic social ideals located in the commodification of ontological difference, generated from and reproducing neoliberal values. We see this when, without irony, the same voices denigrate newly visible political majorities who, their voices having now surfaced *en masse* in public discourse for the first time, are made visible through a public imago—the figure of the enfranchised citizen—that is genuinely authentic, in that it externalizes and is expressive of a worldview that was previously held in private or denied public expression. The hypocrisy that lies in liberal democratic espousing of the value of authenticity, while simultaneously attacking precisely that authentic self-expression in others, exposes its premise and utility as an ideological tool to sustain neoliberal ontological economization. If the invocation of the locker room not only reserves the right to certain speech but also allows the appearance and entrance into public political discourse of that which would otherwise be prohibited from it, the figuration was used as well in an appeal to a silent majority who were ostensibly given voice through the Trump campaign.

In his psychoanalytic study of silence, *A Voice and Nothing More* (2005), Mladen Dolar scrutinizes the politics of the voice in contemporary life and configures the spectacle of modern democracies—the rallies, the speeches, the cheering and the debates—as platforms that give expression to competing political voices. Recent debates over the right to free speech versus no-platforming evidence the continuing importance of the voice within Western democracy, as does the establishment of hermetic spaces within campus life, known as safe spaces, that form ideological lacunae and are constituted as spaces of physical and psychic removal from the voice of the other. From a Freudian position, it is difficult to argue for such a muting of public debate. The late Freud codifies the unconscious as silent; it is the ego that speaks, and the role of psychoanalysis, as of his and Breuer's discovery of free association—the cornerstone of the entire psychoanalytic project—is structured on a principle that the unconscious be accessed via the voice. From the case study that launched psychoanalysis, that of Anna O., silence, or the refusal to speak, was understood to be a symptom of repression, and the therapeutic responsibility of the analyst to give voice to that which could not be said or was gestured to only via non-verbal means. As testified through Anna O's polyglotism that gave way to silence and also through Dora's refusal to speak, psychoanalysis is predicated on a need to give articulation, to listen to and interpret memories that have been psychically repressed by the ego. Both sides of the current dispute over free speech can be interpreted as symptoms of a modern neurosis linked to the role that the voice occupies in contemporary life, and yet a program of institutional silencing works in the favor of the dominant social order. The locker room and safe space share in common the perception that the external environment is repressive. For advocates of the safe space, it constitutes a retreat from dominant, even dangerous, intersectionally oppressive structurations and the inequalities they propagate. For Trump, the locker room provides a retreat from the social injunctions of multicultural liberal democracy. They differ in their relation to the aural and oral: while the former is a space of articulation predicated on censorship of competing voices through removal, the latter is one of delayed expression, where self-silencing and self-censorship are set aside.

Discussion in the aftermath of both the Brexit referendum in the United Kingdom and Trump election in the United States relied on the metaphor of a silent majority to rationalize results that defied the predictions of psephologists. As Mladen Dolar states, silence is integral to the polling booth:

> [t]he electoral voice has to be a silent voice (a silenced voice): it has to be given by writing (by crossing or encircling), and it has to be performed in a small cabin, a cell-like cubicle, in complete isolation (in French it is actually called *l'isoloir*), in complete silence.[45]

For Dolar, that voting demands phonic silence underscored by a graphic inscription illustrates the suppression of the threat posed to ideological authority by the collective voice: 'it has to be done one by one, so that the collective outburst of the acclamatory voice is broken down, nipped in the bud, seemingly deprived of its essential qualities and its spectacular effects'.[46] Silence reveals the injunction to obedience demanded by the dominant order *and* the way in which the logic of power comes to infiltrate the minds of subjects. Dolar nonetheless finds a quiet cause for optimism, for although the act of voting represents a voice 'measured and counted, the voice submitted to arithmetic, the voice entrusted to a written sign, a mute voice deprived of any sonority' it is, he argues, 'still a voice'.[47] In the case of Trump's locker room, the space undergoes another metamorphosis to become the polling booth; in it the silent majority, a dormant and previously depoliticized constituency, are able to express their views.

As instructive as Dolar's work is on silence, it cannot fully account for the way in which silence operates in an era where politics has become defined by rage. When the polling booth becomes a locker room, it reconstitutes a collective voice that finds articulation in the act of casting a vote. The booth is also the alternative safe space, where both self-silencing and muting by social prohibition give way under a repressed frustration that reimagines the voting booth as a place offering a very pure form of psychic liberation wherein the repressive strictures of modernity are removed and where individuals are free to express both rational and irrational fears, angers, worries, hatreds and obscenities. Following another formulation found in the pages of the late Freud, discontentment spreads among the masses proportionally to the increase in civilization required to keep their libidinal lives in check; however, this dissatisfaction requires channeling and, subsequently, manipulation by a leader figure who possesses the ability to ventriloquize the voice of the collective to facilitate the necessary political change. Such a process suggests that late capitalism brings two intellectual components of late Freud into conflict with each other: the dictatorship of reason and the leader's power to manipulate mass psychology.

In *Group Psychology and the Analysis of the Ego*, Freud sets out a psychoanalytic theory of the leader and his ability to manipulate libidinal desire at an individual level to forge a psychology of the masses. Once again Freud's proclamation that psychoanalysis, as a science, should refuse to adopt a *Weltanschuuang*, even a political one, is undermined by the two key words contained within the title, 'group psychology' and 'ego'; these terms make manifest the truth that psychoanalysis was never solely concerned with the individual, but always with the individual within a wider social structure. In fact, the more insistent Freud's disavowing of politics becomes in the later work, the more such utterances begin to resemble the sort of rhetorical devices employed by his patients. Freud teaches us that the unconscious does not want to be found or accessed, but instead retreats from view only to be accessed by way of a period of sustained analysis. Unconscious desires are displaced or re-cathected, in ways that resemble Freud's reluctance to confront the political dimensions latent within his own psychoanalytic project; by denying the political dimension coded within psychoanalysis, Freud attempts to erect a false distinction between the public and private that is undermined by his work. Although the analysand is encouraged to retreat from the public when stepping into the consulting room—the Wolfman, for example, described the experience of walking into Freud's room as both spatially and temporally an uncanny one—the entire exchange is predicated on the idea that after the fifty minutes expire, the subject will once again take their place within society. We only have to recall the criticism levelled by the anti-psychiatry movement against psychoanalysis, namely that it had become adopted as a form of statecraft which had imposed set thresholds of normative behavior upon citizens, to be reminded of the psychoanalytic importance of the individual within the social. Freud highlights the way in which the two terms of his title are directly implicated in his opening remarks to *Group Psychology*, when he writes that:

> It is true that individual psychology is concerned with the individual man and explores the paths by which he seeks to find satisfaction for his instinctual impulses; but only rarely and under certain exceptional conditions is individual psychology in a position to disregard the relations of this individual to others. In the individual's mental life someone else is invariably involved, as a model, as an object, as a helper, as an opponent; and so from the very first individual psychology, in this extended but entirely justifiable sense of the words, is at the same time social psychology as well.[48]

In *Group Psychology* Freud expands upon an idea first introduced in the earlier *On Narcissism*: that the ego undergoes a process of splintering in childhood during the process of Oedipal identification with the parent of the same sex and that this event is accompanied by a quota of hostility on account of the thwarting of narcissistic desires in the formation of what the later Freud terms in *Group Psychology* the 'ego-ideal'. As Freud remarks, 'we have been driven to the hypothesis that some such agency develops in our ego which may cut itself off from the rest of the ego and come into conflict with it'.[49] This phenomenon is often schematized as that part of the superego that houses impossible images of self-perfection; the dicta propagated by the beauty, fashion and self-help industries, Instagram affirmations of being the best 'you' possible or the 'you' that you have always dreamed of being. It is in *Group Psychology* that Freud designates the ego-ideal as an autonomous psychic apparatus with origins in the complicated Oedipal phenomenon of infantile narcissism (the object-cathexis towards desired parent) and the child's identification with the collective ideals of father. Clearly differentiated from both the ego and the superego, the ego-ideal (born out of the conflict between idealization and identification) is developed into a theory to accommodate the behaviors of the individual in a group. Freud provides a topological graphic of his collective ego-ideal theory, a diagrammatic imagining outlining how '*a number of individuals* [...] *have put one and the same object in the place of their ego ideal and have consequently identified themselves with one another in their ego*'.[50] Freud nominates first the primal father, and then the political leader, as the figure who occupies the position of the outer object: 'the primal father is the group ideal, which governs the ego in place of the ego ideal'.[51] It is here, then, that Freud's theorizing of group psychology begins to explain the rise of charismatic leaders who provide a psychic conduit that allows individuals within a mass to experience a vicarious identification with the leader figure. Freud's work on group psychology—and it is important to stress that the model of leadership expounded therein is one of which he disapproved—explicates the emergence of an individual like Trump, whose electoral success can, in part, be explained in the ways that he has colonized the space of group ego-ideal as the leader figure who gives voice to desires, fears and wishes deemed too shameful by the cultural superego of twenty-first century modernity.

Once again outlining psychoanalysis as a system of thought that is inherently concerned with the relation of the individual to the collective, Freud provides a predictive description of the current President of the United States in his sketch of the primal father who would presage the Nietzschean *Übermensch*:

> Individual psychology must, on the contrary, be just as old as group psychology, for from the first there were two kinds of psychologies, that of the individual members of the group and that of the father, chief, or leader. The members of the group were subject to ties just as we see them today, but the father of the primal horde was free. His intellectual acts were strong and independent even in isolation, and his will needed no reinforcement from others. Consistency leads us to assume that his ego had few libidinal ties; he loved no one but himself, or other people only in so far as they served his needs.[52]

To address the question of whether Trump's election represents a crisis in democracy: on the one hand it does not, in the constitutional and legal sense, because enough of the demos exercised its right to elect him into office; however, Freud's psychoanalytic formation of group psychology and its relationship to desire make clear the threat to the very possibility of democracy (even in its imperfect formulation) in an age of mass democracy. Though, as Brown has shown, neoliberal rationality goes far beyond the opportunities afforded by political office by undoing the conditions of democracy as it is predicated on social bonds, political populism on either the far right or far left makes a virtue of economic non-sense in the propagation of alternative, emotive value systems. If for Marx any moment is loaded with infinite forms of possibility, this purportedly new form of politics offers no such possibility, deriving reactively from and further entrenching the dominant system that it appears whether inadvertently or complicitly to eschew, rather than emerging as an alternative to its undoing. For psychoanalysis, every intimate emotional relationship (marital, familial, paternal) is believed to contain an element of resentment or hostility towards the love object that remains under the radar of consciousness as a result of repression: this is the well-known ambivalence mobilized constantly in the psychoanalytic method. The same phenomenon occurs for Freud when individuals come together in the formation of collective identities. Freud states how those imagined communities, in closest proximity, harbor the most hostility towards one another (which he will later refer to as the 'narcissism of minor differences'), citing as examples the ferocity of feeling between Scots and English, Spanish and Portuguese.[53] This ambivalence is discernible in the semiotics of the Trumpian maxim, 'Build the Wall': an exclusionary message counter to the historical tradition of America as a country of immigration, but a nativist idea in which an American essentialism is forged in opposition to neighboring nation states.

Trump's attempts to connect nativism and nationalism appeal to economic foundations, but are indicative of the sort of leader about whom Freud writes in *Group Psychology*. Neoliberal economic orthodoxy, aligned to liberal democracy, is turned on its head in favor of the act of binding people together in ever closer, isolationist bonds, achieved through a familiar process of scapegoating and exclusionism. If group formation is facilitated by a re-cathexis of love away from a traditional love object (the sexual figure of desire) and directed to the figure of the leader who in turn uses it to foster a strong identification with a group, then this reworking of desire into a political process results in an erosion of freedom. An irony begins to emerge within that primal horde of Trump supporters who strongly identify with libertarian philosophies of 'free speech', denigrate 'snowflakes' and espouse 'the right to offend', as membership of a group reveals an 'individual's lack of freedom in a group'.[54] Those crying the loudest for 'freedom', therefore, are recast as those under the greatest sway, those most lacking in a singular identity and most intolerant to those belonging to group identities other to their own; whether or not Trump in fact shares these ideological principles or merely capitalizes on them to advance his own globalized agenda becomes irrelevant. Freud speculates that when the hostility present in the ambivalence of love is cultured in the formation of groups born out of intolerance to neighbors, such groupings are ironically the most tolerant of difference within that same group itself. This would then allow the Ivy League-educated businessman to vote for the same political leader as the uneducated male from Arkansas; as Freud observes: '[s]o long as a group formation persists or so far as it extends, individuals in the group behave as though they were uniform, tolerate the peculiarities of its other members, equate themselves with them, and have no feeling of aversion towards them'.[55]

A unifying characteristic of Freud's late work, both in the continued development of his metapsychology and in his social writings, is his belief in a universal drive and tendency towards destruction. It is on account of his discovery of death drive as a psychoanalytic general theory that Freud sanctions the creation of a reasoned elite schooled in the methods of secular statecraft in *The Future of an Illusion*, but consistent with his schematizing of death drive in the late texts, Freud was unable to fully comprehend the consequences of his social theory. Human aggressiveness and a tendency towards violence required the imposition of an organizational elite in order to safeguard against the threat posed to civilization itself. What Freud was unable to foresee, however, is how a political leader like Trump would embody his theoretical work on mass psychology effectively to mobilize against this Freudian dictatorship of reason. *The Future of an Illusion* and *Group Psychology* are thus brought into conflict with each other via the figure of the populist leader, who in the twenty-first century has made an enemy of the experts.[56]

In the final pages of *Civilization and Its Discontents* Freud provides an ominous portrait of a despotic leader figure, often considered to be a veiled representation of Hitler:

> The super-ego of an epoch of civilization has an origin similar to that of an individual. It is based on the impression left behind by the personalities of great leaders—men of overwhelming force of mind in whom one of the human impulsions has found its strongest and purest, and therefore often its most one-sided, expression. In many instances the analogy goes still further, in that during their lifetime these figures were—often enough, even if not always—mocked and maltreated by others and even dispatched in a cruel fashion.[57]

While critical attention has remained focused on the sway of 'great leaders' to give shape to their own and subsequent epochs, less has been made of Freud's muted warning on how dissenting voices should engage with such leader figures. The Freudian antidote to this Freudian leader is to treat Trump as the socio-political symptom, with its originary neurosis in the iniquitous distribution of capital in the twentieth and twenty-first centuries. Freud instructs us that jokes are rarely a laughing matter because they possess a relationality with the unconscious, so it follows that the caricaturing of Trump as a bad joke of a President fails to recognize both the complicated desires that led to his election and its historical formations in liberal democracy. The mocking of Trump carries the risk of heightening perceptions of his continued maltreatment at the hands of an established political class and an international mainstream media supported by liberal voters in coastal metropolitan constituencies and estranged from the lives of a majority of American citizens. As morally and politically objectionable as figures such as Trump are experienced to be on the Western political stage, should the perception take hold of his being 'dispatched in a cruel fashion', then the 'impression'—as Freud terms it—that he will leave behind, will be that of a residue of even greater discontentment towards democratic procedures and institutions.

Here we are reminded once again of the closing section of *The Future of an Illusion* and its controversial focus on religion, which is largely structured in the final pages of the text in terms of a Platonic Dialogue. Towards the end of the book he replies to his imagined interlocutor—who is established as a champion of religion, religious life and religious education as the primary means to maintain civilization—by acknowledging, in typically Freudian fashion, that his findings may indeed be wrong, that the psychologist's work may not apply to the socio-historical, but that 'the weakness of my position does not imply any strength of yours. I think you are defending a lost cause'.[58] Freud's performed objectivity (for he clearly believes in the reasoned veracity of his findings) provides a signal means to think about the bifurcated politics of today. This chapter has identified Freud as an underacknowledged architect of the politics of the early twenty-first century, but his work also provides a possible way out of the current moment. At its most basic, psychoanalysis is a communal enterprise that demands the intersubjectivity of another; its dynamics are mutual. The importance of the Freudian methodology persists—where jokes are taken seriously, where locker room chat is given vocal expression and where it is recognized that safe spaces, like the clinic, are also social. Neurotic voices need to be listened to in all of their contradictions.

Notes

1. See Chap. 5 for a full discussion of the IPA as the political wing of Freudian psychoanalysis.
2. Mladen Dolar, 'Freud and the Political', *Harvard Journal of the Legal Left*, Vol. 4:15 (2008), pp. 15–29 (17).
3. Ibid.
4. See Joel Whitebook, *Perversion and Utopia: A Study in Psychoanalysis and Critical Theory* (Cambridge, MA and London: The MIT Press, 1995).
5. Sigmund Freud, *New Introductory Lectures on Psycho-Analysis*, in *The Standard Edition of the Complete Psychological Works of Sigmund Freud*, trans. by James Strachey, Vol. XXII (London: Hogarth Press, 1964c [1933]), pp. 5–182 (181).
6. Sigmund Freud, *The Future of an Illusion*, in *The Standard Edition of the Complete Psychological Works of Sigmund Freud*, trans. by James Strachey, Vol. XXI (London: Hogarth Press, 1964d [1927]), pp. 5–56 (6).
7. Freud (1964d, p. 6).
8. Freud (1964d, p. 7).
9. Freud (1964d, p. 6).
10. Freud (1964d, pp. 7–8).
11. Freud (1964d, p. 43). Freud develops this theory more fully in *Moses and Monotheism*, where he consciously grafts in the language of psychoanalytic practice—early trauma, repression, latency, partial return of repressed memory—to explain the historical development of civilization from ancient Egypt to early twentieth-century Europe.
12. Freud (1964d, p. 51).
13. Freud (1964d, p. 49).
14. Freud (1964d, p. 8).
15. In *Civilization and Its Discontents,* he would revise this idea slightly in presenting his formulation that happiness is directly proportional to the amount of civilization that is experienced.
16. Ernest Jones, *The Young Freud, 1856-1900 – The Life and Work of Sigmund Freud*, Vol. I (London: Hogarth Press, 1957), p. 180. See also Paul Roazen, *The Trauma of Freud: Controversies in Psychoanalysis* (New Brunswick, NJ: Transaction Publishers, 2002) for discussion of the translation and Mussolini's response, and Paul Roazen, *Edoardo Weiss: The House That Freud Built* (New Brunswick, NJ: Transaction Publishers, 2005) for further discussion of Freud and Mussolini. For a more detailed discussion of psychoanalysis and Italian fascism see Mauro Pasqualini, 'Origin, Rise and Destruction of Psychoanalytic Culture in Fascist Italy, 1922-1937' in *Psychoanalysis and Politics: Histories of Psychoanalysis Under Conditions of*

Restricted Political Freedom, ed. by Joy Damousi and Mariano Ben Plotkin (Oxford: Oxford University Press, 2012), pp. 7–35.

17. Sigmund Freud, *Moses and Monotheism: Three Essays*, in *The Standard Edition of the Complete Psychological Works of Sigmund Freud*, trans. by James Strachey, Vol. XXIII (London: Hogarth Press, 1964e [1939]), pp. 7–137 (54).
18. Freud (1964e, p. 54).
19. Freud (1964e, p. 54).
20. Sigmund Freud and Albert Einstein, *Why War?*, in *The Standard Edition of the Complete Psychological Works of Sigmund Freud,* trans. by James Strachey, Vol. XXII (London: Hogarth Press, 1964f [1933]), pp. 197–219 (212).
21. Freud (1964f, p. 213).
22. Freud (1964b, p. 111).
23. See Wendy Brown, *Undoing the Demos: Neoliberalism's Stealth Revolution* (New York, NY: Zone Books, 2015).
24. Freud (1964d, p. 7).
25. Freud (1964d, p. 8).
26. Freud (1964d, p. 12).
27. Freud (1964d, p. 13).
28. Ibid.
29. Freud (1964d, p. 13).
30. Sigmund Freud, *Analysis Terminable and Interminable*, in *The Standard Edition of the Complete Psychological Works of Sigmund Freud*, trans. by James Strachey, Vol. XXIII (London: Hogarth Press, 1964g [1937]), pp. 216–53 (248).
31. Freud (1964g, pp. 250–1).
32. Freud (1964g, pp. 219–20).
33. See Mark Blyth, *Austerity: The History of a Dangerous Idea* (Oxford: Oxford University Press, 2013), p. 115. In *Austerity: The History of a Dangerous Idea* (2013) Mark Blyth cites Angela Merkel's evocation of a figurative Swabian *hausfrau* as it was used to legitimate her government's austerity agenda. The German Chancellor's language reveals the superego power of the state to rule by guilt when presenting the fiscal responsibility of Europe's most powerful country in terms of a maternal superego.
34. Michael Gove, cited in 'Britain Has Had Enough of Experts', *The Financial Times*, June 3 2016.
35. Ibid.
36. 'Transcript: Donald Trump's Taped Comments About Women', *The New York Times*, October 8 2016.
37. 'Transcript of the Second Debate', *The New York Times*, October 10 2016.
38. 'Transcript of the Second Debate', *The New York Times*, October 10 2016.

39. 'Transcript of the Second Debate', *The New York Times*, October 10 2016.
40. 'Transcript of the Second Debate', *The New York Times*, October 10 2016.
41. This tension is discernible in Robert Mueller's investigation into collusion with Russia during the campaign, 'The Cohen Tapes' and the ongoing rumor that the Kremlin possesses incriminating video evidence involving Trump.
42. Slavoj Žižek, *Living in the End Times* (London: Verso, 2010), p. 324.
43. Žižek (2010, pp. 323–4).
44. Slavoj Žižek, 'Berlusconi in Tehran', *The London Review of Books*, Vol. 21. No. 14, July 23 (2009), pp. 3–7.
45. Mladen Dolar, *A Voice and Nothing More* (Cambridge, MA and London: MIT Press, 2005), p. 112.
46. Dolar (2005, p. 112).
47. Dolar (2005, p. 112).
48. Sigmund Freud, *Group Psychology and the Analysis of the Ego*, in *The Standard Edition of the Complete Psychological Works of Sigmund Freud*, trans. by James Strachey, Vol. XVIII (London: Hogarth Press, 1955b [1921]), pp. 68–143 (69).
49. Freud (1955b, p. 109).
50. Freud (1955b, p. 115).
51. Freud (1955b, p. 127).
52. Freud (1955b, p. 123).
53. Freud (1964b, p. 114).
54. Freud (1955b, p. 94).
55. Freud (1955b, p. 102).
56. Todd McGowan too identifies the cultivation of a mistrust of experts as a signature feature of right-wing populism, observing in *Enjoying What We Don't Have: The Political Project of Psychoanalysis* (2013) that while 'the traditional master prohibits enjoyment, the populist leader liberates subjects from the restrictions of their enjoyment posed by experts'. Todd McGowan, *Enjoying What We Don't Have: The Political Project of Psychoanalysis* (Lincoln, NE: University of Nebraska, 2013), p. 176.
57. Freud (1964b, p. 141).
58. Freud (1964d, p. 53).

Works Cited

Mark Blyth, *Austerity: The History of a Dangerous Idea* (Oxford: Oxford University Press, 2013).

Wendy Brown, *Undoing the Demos: Neoliberalism's Stealth Revolution* (New York, NY: Zone Books, 2015).

Mladen Dolar, *A Voice and Nothing More* (Cambridge, MA and London: MIT Press, 2005).

Mladen Dolar, 'Freud and the Political', *Harvard Journal of the Legal Left*, Vol. 4:15 (2008).

Sigmund Freud, *Group Psychology and the Analysis of the Ego*, in *The Standard Edition of the Complete Psychological Works of Sigmund Freud*, trans. by James Strachey, Vol. XVIII (London: Hogarth Press, 1955 [1921]).

Sigmund Freud, *Civilization and Its Discontents*, in *The Standard Edition of the Complete Psychological Works of Sigmund Freud*, trans. by James Strachey, Vol. XXI (London: Hogarth Press, 1964 [1930]).

Sigmund Freud, *The Future of an Illusion*, in *The Standard Edition of the Complete Psychological Works of Sigmund Freud*, trans. by James Strachey, Vol. XXI (London: Hogarth Press, 1964 [1927]).

Sigmund Freud, *New Introductory Lectures on Psycho-Analysis*, in *The Standard Edition of the Complete Psychological Works of Sigmund Freud*, trans. by James Strachey, Vol. XXII (London: Hogarth Press, 1964 [1933]).

Sigmund Freud and Albert Einstein, *Why War?*, in *The Standard Edition of the Complete Psychological Works of Sigmund Freud*, trans. by James Strachey, Vol. XXII (London: Hogarth Press, 1964 [1933]).

Sigmund Freud, *Analysis Terminable and Interminable*, in *The Standard Edition of the Complete Psychological Works of Sigmund Freud*, trans. by James Strachey, Vol. XXIII (London: Hogarth Press, 1964 [1937]).

Sigmund Freud, *Moses and Monotheism: Three Essays*, in *The Standard Edition of the Complete Psychological Works of Sigmund Freud*, trans. by James Strachey, Vol. XXIII (London: Hogarth Press, 1964 [1939]).

Ernest Jones, *The Young Freud, 1856–1900 – The Life and Work of Sigmund Freud*, Vol. I (London: Hogarth Press, 1957).

Todd McGowan, *Enjoying What We Don't Have: The Political Project of Psychoanalysis* (Lincoln, NE: University of Nebraska, 2013).

Joel Whitebook, *Perversion and Utopia: A Study in Psychoanalysis and Critical Theory* (Cambridge, MA and London: The MIT Press, 1995).

Slavoj Žižek, 'Berlusconi in Tehran', *The London Review of Books*, Vol. 21. No. 14, July 23 (2009).

Slavoj Žižek, *Living in the End Times* (London: Verso, 2010).

CHAPTER 3

(Psycho)Social Media

> In the course of centuries the *naïve* self-love of men has had to submit to two major blows at the hands of science. The first was when they learnt that our earth was not the center of the universe but only a tiny fragment of a cosmic system of scarcely imaginable vastness. This is associated with Copernicus [...] The second blow fell when biological research destroyed man's supposedly privileged place in creation and proved his descent from the animal kingdom and his ineradicable animal nature. This revaluation has been accomplished in our own days by Darwin [...] though not without the most violent contemporary opposition. But human megalomania will have suffered its third and most wounding blow from the psychological research of the present time which seeks to prove to the ego that it is not even master in its own house, but must content itself with scanty information of what is going on unconsciously in its mind.[1]

Freud's Social Network

In a book that concentrates on the works from the late era of Freud's intellectual life, the quotation that frames this chapter is one of the most oft-cited by supporters and critics of Freud alike. Positioning himself within a constellation of intellectual disruptors, Freud outlines the ways in which the advent of psychoanalysis represents a mortal blow to the narcissism of humanity. Freud's presentation of psychoanalysis as a fixed and empirical body of scientific research belies the potential of several of the discoveries that fall within our designation of his late period to compromise the

M.-D. Dick, R. McLaughlan, *Late Capitalist Freud in Literary, Cultural, and Political Theory*,
https://doi.org/10.1007/978-3-030-47194-1_3

entirety of the psychoanalytic project. Theoretical developments such as death drive and his intellectual move from a topographical towards a structural model of the unconscious are presented to his reader as refinements to already well-established psychoanalytic principles. In truth, and especially with the publication of *Beyond the Pleasure Principle* in 1920, many of Freud's late discoveries threatened to undermine the discipline constructed as his life's work. His belief in psychoanalysis as a third epistemological revolution following on from those of Copernicus and Darwin now appears, to the critics of psychoanalysis, to be naïve at best and premature at worst. We argue that the decentering of the subject it effected is now being undone by a fourth revolution, that of the tech age, which seeks to reinstall the subject at the center of the universe even as it harnesses the unconscious in order to do so.

In this chapter we posit the underacknowledged social significance of Freud's shift from a vision of the psyche based on spatiality to one of competing agents and examine how this diagrammatic vision of the psyche places greater emphasis on the external world in the role of personality formation. The second finding of this chapter is that the advent of social media technology has facilitated a development in the historiography of one of Freud's most significant late discoveries: the superego. In what follows we suggest that the rise of social media can be interpreted in relation to its psychoanalytic dimensions: the first section outlines a proto-theory of the psychosocial network as set out in Freud, while the second and third sections employ Facebook and Instagram as case studies to uncover the legacy of the late Freud in the tech age, read as a neoliberal formation. This chapter advances the discoveries presented by Freud in *The Ego and the Id* and extends this late text into the digital era of late capitalism.

The political shift that defines Freud's late theorizing of the individual within wider social life belies how from its very inception psychoanalysis was the most social of sciences. Throughout his life Freud retained an interest in ancient civilizations; his consultation room in Vienna housed a collection of historical artefacts, testifying to the way in which he conceived of psychoanalysis as a form of psychic archaeology. Freud's fascination with the classical world went beyond a mere aesthetic appreciation; instead, his interest in archaeology was methodological and evidenced a world view of life predicated upon the unseen ruins of previous eras. In an extended analogy from an early publication, Freud imaginatively overlays the socio-anthropological onto the individual when discussing the way in which the psychoanalytic method doubles as a form of personal archaeology: in 'The Aetiology of Hysteria' (1896) Freud invites his audience to follow him on an intellectual excursus, describing an unknown explorer who stumbles upon the ruins of a 'semi-barbaric' civilization and then sets out to decode the mysteries that confront him. In order to make sense of his contemporary moment, Freud stages a cultural encounter between a figure of European intellectual modernity and a non-European society, suggesting that the explorer/analyst figure must seek the co-operation of the people and turn their attention to what lies beneath the surface:

> Together with them he may start upon the ruins, clear away the rubbish, and, beginning from the visible remains, uncover what is buried. If his work is crowned with success, the discoveries are self-explanatory: the ruined walls are part of the ramparts of a palace or a treasure-house; the fragments of columns can be filled out into a temple; the numerous inscriptions, which, by good luck, may be bilingual, reveal an alphabet and a language, and, when they have been deciphered and translated, yield undreamed-of-information about the events of the remote past, to commemorate which the monuments were built. *Saxa loquuntur!*[2]

Here Freud's belief that the unconscious is a vast archive of memory—nothing is ever forgotten—coheres with a belief that the modern world is built upon the ruins of previous civilizations.[3]

In 'Excavation and Memory' (1923), Walter Benjamin observes that '[h]e who seeks to approach his own buried past must conduct himself like a man digging'.[4] Benjamin extends the archaeological comparison in a metaphor that echoes that previously used by Freud to describe the psychoanalytic process: '[a]bove all, he must not be afraid to return again and again to the same matter; to scatter it as one scatters earth, to turn it over as one turns over soil'.[5] The archaeological is here melded with the geological, yet both the Freudian and Benjaminian analogies describe the process of self-understanding as necessitating a quite literal process of self-discovery. This is precisely the image of the unconscious that emerges in another of the late Freud's essays, 'A Note upon the "Mystic Writing Pad"' (1925), in which he turns to capitalist commodity culture to provide a diagrammatic exposition of memory as it is stored within his configuration of the mind. A Freudian anticipation of Apple's iPad, the Mystic Writing Pad was a popular toy in early twentieth-century Europe that allowed users (in this case, infants) to write upon an erasable screen, just as a modern tablet or smartphone does today, using a stylus to inscribe upon a celluloid surface that could then be wiped clean by pulling up the top sheet covering a wax tablet underneath. The toy permitted the child to doodle or to write and then, by lifting the paper and film, to erase the marks that appeared on the surface and begin the process of reinscription. Yet what captures Freud's theoretical imagination is the unseen engineering of the toy, and in this essay he metaphorically breaks its mechanisms apart to analyze how the writing pad's functionality mirrors the architecture of the unconscious. Freud uses the mechanics of the toy to sketch out a relationship between the external world and a process of internal recording: '[o]n the Mystic Pad the writing vanishes every time the close contact is broken between the paper which receives the stimulus and the wax slab which preserves the impression'.[6] This observation also operates on an archaeological model: nothing is lost to the mystic writing pad, which preserves the traces of inscription on its waxy substrate even as the subject preserves the traces of experience on the unconscious.

Yet this archaeological/geological allegorizing of psychoanalysis by Freud himself, his followers, and even his critics did not mean that psychoanalysis was a stable, fixed—fossilized even—body of work. Just as Freud was convinced that the modern world and the classical world exist not in isolation but in continuum, we contend that the work of the late Freud remains a latent theoretical force that underpins late capitalism as an organizational system and the cultural production that emerges alongside it. In the latter years of his life Freud was always keen when presenting a new idea to portray such configurations as advancements of earlier ideas, as opposed to radical ruptures. For much of its history during Freud's lifetime, psychoanalytic theory imagined the psyche in terms of three lines of division: preconscious, conscious and the unconscious. Yet this rendering of the unconscious continued to testify, albeit subtly, to the importance of the external world in the history of personality formation at the level of the individual. The pleasure principle represents the primal discovery of early Freudian psychoanalysis, from which so many of his later discoveries would originate. Equally important to the developmental history of psychoanalysis was Freud's theorizing of a counteractive force whose aim is to check the id's injunction to pleasure; this, of course, was given the name of the reality principle. The id is the only component, both in the topographical and the later structural model, that is present from birth.[7] Unlike the id, the ego is the consequence of the infant's realization that it is a social being and as such, that its desires need to be checked to bring it in line with established social behavior. Freud stresses the *social* dimension to his theory of psychosocial development in *The Ego and the Id* when writing that:

> the ego seeks to bring the influence of the external world to bear upon the id and its tendencies, and endeavors to substitute the reality principle for the pleasure principle which reigns unrestrictedly in the id. For the ego, perception plays the part which in the id falls to instinct. The ego represents what may be called reason and common sense, in contrast to the id, which contains the passions.[8]

Here Freud identifies the ego as ordered by an understanding of those social rules and prohibitions that are presented as constituting 'common sense'. Although Freud does not spend any time developing this ideological dimension to ego formation, the ego's alignment with common sense provides a subtle insight into how individual personality formation could be manipulated by external agents and influences. Common sense as understood by Freud, then, represents a set of behaviors that adheres to the dominant social equilibrium. The ego owes its very existence to the external actors and the injunctions they demand, becoming internalized within the mind of the subject. This idea of common sense as aligned with the logic of a governing doxa has been brought into theoretical focus more recently by David Harvey when he writes that 'Neoliberalism [...] has pervasive effects on ways of thought to the point where it has become incorporated into the common-sense way many of us interpret, live in, and understand the world'.[9] Wendy Brown goes beyond Harvey, borrowing from a Freudian language to assert how neoliberalism *is* the world as experienced by contemporary subjects: '[n]eoliberalism governs as sophisticated common sense, a reality principle remaking institutions and human beings everywhere it settles, nestles, and gains affirmation'.[10] The importance of society in psyche formation, albeit much less pronounced than in the later work, complicates the received timeline that designates the political shift within the work of the late Freudian canon, suggesting that Freud's association of the ego with a logic of common sense reveals a public dimension to his work even in the apparent concentration on the individual within the early writing. As discussed in the previous chapter, *Civilization and Its Discontents* demonstrates that individuals do not live in isolation but find security in social networks, and Freud's theorizing of individual psychic formation establishes that this process always occurs within a wider social grouping. This, in turn, means that those who shape the external world possess a great power to shape the unconscious desires of subjects who live under their reach.

The structural shift in the late Freud is characterized by a movement from a configuration of the psyche in terms of spaces (the topographical model) to a configuration wherein conflict is generated by means of different agencies (the structural model). As such, Freud's psychosocial theory of personality development is complicated yet further in his body of late work, in which he schematizes individual psyche development as an interconnected psychosocial network of influences. Freud himself appears confused as to what this theoretical shift from the topographical to the structural model means for psychoanalysis. In the editorial note that accompanies his translation of *The Ego and the Id* in the *Standard Edition*, James Strachey asserts that the 'new terminology' adopted by Freud 'had a highly clarifying effect and so made further clinical advances possible', yet stresses that this move from a system of spatiality to one of competing agents 'did not in itself involve any fundamental changes in Freud's views on mental structure and functioning'.[11] Freud offers a more contradictory appraisal. While repeatedly stating that this shift towards a structural understanding simply represented a foregrounding of that which was latently implied in the model that had underpinned psychoanalytic theory for most of its existence, the emergent importance of 'guilt' within his argument led to the introduction of a psychic apparatus—the superego—referred to by Freud as a '*new* discovery'.[12]

Crucially, this third psychic agent—whether a new player or not—demonstrates the fundamental role that external influences play in the psychosexual stages of infantile development. *The Ego and the Id* outlines a temporal development in the acquisition of the apparatuses that structure the psychic lives of individuals: we are born into the world as pre-Oedipal figures of unconscious libidinality and then acquire a regulating entity in line with the reality principle, with the ultimate legacy of the Oedipal stage being the internalization of external figures of prohibition. The superego originates from the infant subject's Oedipal interactions with that sovereign figure of prohibition, the father. The 'revolutionary moment' of superego formation, as Freud designates it, occurs as a result of the father figure's warning against an incestuous desire for the mother, which sequentially enacts a fissure within the ego. The creation of the superego is the legacy of the Oedipal stage in psychosexual development towards maturation. The structural model, and Freud's diagrammatic schematizing of it, makes clear how the superego is 'intimately connected' to the id as 'the heir of the Oedipus complex'.[13] The child's Oedipal desire for the mother is thwarted in this psychic drama by the figure of the father—interpretable as both literally the father or a composite form of various authority figures—who is 'perceived as the obstacle to a realization of his Oedipus wishes'.[14] When sketching out the psychic transmigration of father internalized as superego, Freud's work is interpretable as an anticipatory form of social network theory wherein individual development is formed by interacting with a network of influences and social actors. The late work emphasizes how the individual and the collective exist in symbiotic communication, as for example in *The Ego and the Id* wherein Freud reconceives of the human body as a system of detection, translation and sublimation and of human beings as the nodal points of a sensory network of perception within this structural model. Human textures are reworked to become phenomenological technologies that receive and then transmit signals to the unconscious. Our skin, according to Freud, is the site on which the technologies of the senses converge, the 'place from which both external and internal perceptions may spring. It is *seen* like any other object, but to the *touch* it yields two kinds of sensations, one of which may be equivalent to an internal perception'.[15]

Before the sort of psychodynamic investigations that Freud undertook into the origins of civilization, and the instating of what he would come to classify as the cultural superego, his conception of the superego as an external figure or figures that become internalized depicts the external world as a site of regulation and social injunction which exists in perpetual conflict with the impulses and desires originating from the id:

> As a child grows up, the role of the father is carried on by teachers and others in authority; their injunctions and prohibitions remain powerful in the ego ideal and continue, in the form of conscience, to exercise moral censorship. The tension between the demands of conscience and the actual performances of the ego is experienced as a sense of guilt. Social feelings rest on identifications with other people, on the basis of having the same ego ideal.[16]

As argued in the previous chapter, the late Freud began to advocate for the installation of a supranational psychoanalytic elite to maintain global relations; the creation of this governing class was a refinement of Freud's idea of a cultural superego. In *Civilization and Its Discontents* he begins his discussion of the cultural superego by way of an examination of the ideological and epistemic legacy that 'great leaders—men of overwhelming force of mind'—exerted on the societies that survived after their deaths.[17] The moral authority of these leaders shaped the morality of the governing cultural superego. The installation within the psychic lives of all citizens of a system of ethics innately regarded as common sense provides a heretofore underdeveloped glimpse into the importance that Freud invested in the community of men trained in reason that he elects to be the custodians of capitalist democracy. Guilt and shame, the key words of superego that rule within the individual psyche, are replaced with concepts of morality and ethics at the level of community. Whereas in *Group Psychology and the Analysis of the Ego* the late Freud concentrated on individual psychic behavior within a larger social group—in other words, on how repressed feelings are cathected into leader figures or transposed across the mass—Freud's theorizing of a cultural superego interrogates the means by which the libidinal desires of subjects need to be sacrificed in the interest of the greater social good. Our work extends this historical development of the superego from the individual to the social to argue for the existence of a developed psychic force within contemporary life: the cyber superego.

The Cyber Superego

When Mark Zuckerberg states that Facebook provides people with 'a powerful new tool for staying connected to the people they love, for making their voices heard and for building communities and businesses', he emphasizes sharing, relationality and expansion as the end of the social network, highlighting its ability to connect individuals in a way that has been previously not just impossible but inconceivable, creating not only a mode of communication but a system of interconnectivity that alters human relations and society.[18] In this formation of its purpose, social media has to be both instrumentalized and moralized: at once serving affective, political and market ends, but configured as a tool in service rather than an active agent, and moreover as a tool that has no transformative power, beyond that benign community mission, over those lives it connects. Disillusioned pioneers of such platforms acknowledge this is not the case; Sean Parker has disavowed Facebook and other apps for the way in which they have gone about 'exploiting a vulnerability in human psychology', and there is a growing body of data on the effect that platforms have in creating gratification loops through dopamine release that rewire our neurocircuitry and reprogram our behavior.[19] These are examples of technology slipping its already illusory confines and of an inability to police a boundary between real and virtual lives that has now already been elided. We propose that there is a psychoanalytic dimension as well as a neuroscientific basis to the social network. Where the first section of this chapter analyzed Freud's schematizing of the psyche as a proto-social network model, in this section we examine how network platforms engage psychic drives and the implications for a Freudian conception of ego and superego development.

On both Facebook and Instagram, the idea is to post content in the form of photographs, video media and text; this content will be liked, shared and function as your connection to a network of 'friends' and 'followers' that expands through apparently organic but actually algorithmic extension. Whether a user is an Instagram influencer, profiting by advertising goods and services through choreographed candids, or a Facebook poster sharing cat memes, each is engaged in a self-imaging for others, a commodification that proceeds from and reproduces a reconception of the self as brand. This marketing of the self expects direct or indirect profit in the form of likes, opportunity and visibility, all forms of financial, cultural and social capital. By conditioning user behavior through the online platform, social media constructs a new relation both to the self and to others.

For Brown, the neoliberal revolution effects a shift from the human conceived as *homo politicus* to a historical form of *homo oeconomicus* conceived as human capital, 'seeking to strengthen its competitive positioning and appreciate its value' in every sphere.[20] In this iteration, Smithian and Benthamite models of entrepreneurialism and utilitarian self-interest are replaced by a paradigm constructed through 'practices of self-investment and attracting investors' and predicated in finance capital.[21] Brown invokes network technology to describe this self-capitalization:

> Whether through social media "followers," "likes," and "retweets," through rankings and ratings for every activity and domain, or through more directly monetized practices, the pursuit of education, training, leisure, reproduction, consumption, and more are increasingly configured as strategic decisions and practices related to enhancing the self's future value.[22]

While Brown utilizes the example of social media technology to metonymize the operation of neoliberal rationality, her systematic analysis focuses on how traditional institutions are reconfigured by that logic rather than on the new sphere of technology. Arguably, though, this sphere is *sui generis* and not one among many, in that the transformation is not merely visible but modelled, effected and accelerated in it. Indeed, if the message of the neoliberal revolution is to be human capital for others, the logic of social media—known to users and non-users alike—inculcates a behavior that, when reiterated, becomes an ontology as it teaches us how to construct, present, and brand ourselves, and to relate to others as similar brand units. The neoliberal rationality from which these platforms emerge is disseminated through the network: platforms such as Facebook and Instagram discipline the self to a model of human capital appreciation that carries over from the virtual platform, spreads virally beyond its users and reconfigures human relation to self and other in both the real and virtual world. We would go so far as to claim that the neoliberal revolution of the human as identified by Brown is mechanized in the social media platform, which succeeds in reproducing the governing logic of self as human capital and in capitalizing the private sphere of human relations through its architecture.

Just as Freud relied on the archaeological metaphor to understand the invisible drives that shape a contemporary moment, the tech platform is itself reliant on a prior architecture, that of the psyche, and on the harnessing of *its* drives. With Facebook and Instagram, people no longer live the present as present; instead, it is experienced only in so far as it exists to be recorded and uploaded. As such, the present is lived after the fact and as commodity: it is experienced on the 'gram. In effect, the experience as it takes place is the ghost of its future happening, confirmed only in the photograph that exists, not as its trace or symbol as in the Mystic Writing Pad, but as the primary experience itself, so that the order is reversed and the event becomes the trace of its image. The social environment from which it emerges becomes a placeholder for the experience as it will happen, a secondary substrate and a deferred marker of its future fruition. This new figuration of experience is itself compromised: transposed to the platform, it transforms the experience into a product to be presented and into a form of capital that accrues to the individual and ultimately bolsters their own incorporation as capital.

Businesses are now engaged in 'curating' environments for Instagram and affirming in doing so that we consciously assess our daily lives according to the marketability of our activities: in a reworking of the metaphysical paradox we might ask whether, if an experience takes place without a smart phone, it has taken place at all?. Life is lived as an abyss of infinite deferral that means that, while one may visit Disneyland in the real world, one can only ever *go there* once one's photographs are uploaded to the platform; the lived experience is a secondary staging of its future legitimation, its return or profit in the form of likes. Experience becomes anterior to itself, and in terms of its significance as an event takes place for the first time when transferred to the platform; it also then becomes posterior, in that the lived experience 'takes place' only after it has happened, through its realization via the visual commodity. Experience as we understand it is twice displaced from itself. Friendship is transformed from a mutual bond and social relation in becoming a market relation, calculated upon an economy of mutual return. In the other direction, this modality of transaction permeates every level of social interaction, both in self-relation and in relation of that self, so transformed, to the world: from understanding sociality and lived experience through the lens of content-production and as a commodity, to leveraging that product within a network wherein the primary purpose of connection is to deliver a measurable approbation that reconfirms the individual as governed by that market logic. Turning experience into product, it metricizes interrelation and self-relation so that societal bonds are transformed into an economy of exchange and profit. The most significant transformation effected by the tech platform is therefore in structuring relations outside of that platform.

If in social media platforms we see an ontological transformation effected via the ego through an altered relation of the individual to experience, we also see a development of the superego into what we term the cyber superego. For Freud, society is the embodiment of the collective superego in all of its unrealistic and prohibitive demands. His diagnosis of social modernity as neurotic—functioning through lack, rather than excess—leads him to suggest that the 'fateful question for the human species' will be to what extent the 'human instinct of aggression and self-destruction' can be mastered and controlled in order to facilitate communal life.[23] Mark Zuckerberg aligned with the Freudian maxim *homo homini lupus* when, wary of the neighbor/stranger, he acted with superego agency in constructing the original Facebook site so that the 'befriending' function operated to include only on the basis of exclusion: the message being, you can be my friend if I allow you to be. The network, however, produces an architectonic development in the superego. While it may be a constricting agent as conceived by Freud—'the price we pay for our advanced civilization', as he writes, 'is a loss of happiness'—when transposed to society, the cultural superego emerges as a vital component in the safeguarding of the collective against the latent aggressive tendencies of the individual.[24] Social media technology has resulted in a reworking of this Freudian formula, whereby the aggression of an anonymous collective is turned back upon the individual. The malevolence of the troll and the follower's praise are two sides of the same (bit)coin, wherein the 'social' aspect of the network functions to direct and internalize a collective pressure upon the social media subject. That pressure is structured as a cyber agency that becomes ever more encompassing as the necessity of accountability is removed and substituted by a code of behaviors and vocabularies—the truncated language and emoji symbols of the tweet, comment or caption.

This altered form can be termed the cyber superego, though within that formulation the term 'cyber' is not synonymous with a retro cyberspace removed from the real. The cyber superego represents the collapse of a false binary distinction between an illusory and formerly sequestered 'cyberspace' so designated and an external reality, distinct and separable from virtual life. In true Freudian style, the cyber superego is not a new idea, but a progression of the form of the superego and, more specifically, of the cultural superego as theorized by Freud. It exists online but escapes its confines, and by so doing fragments the border and the distinction on which that boundary is predicated. As an evolutionary shift in the historiography of the superego this cyber incarnation corresponds with an internalization of superego agency within the minds of users of social networking sites, but we can also observe in it what is, according to Wendy Brown, one of the hallmarks of late capitalism, namely the shift from hard coercive power, wielded through state institutions and centralized authority, to a disseminated soft power, operating through the lexicon of governance, best practice, benchmarks and shared values. Through such techniques Brown argues that the self is made human capital in a particular fashion, according to an economic model filtered through registers of finance capital that transfer market logic into all domains and transform them accordingly: encouraged to conceive of itself 'as both a member of a firm and as itself a firm', the individual is governed by practices geared to securing value appreciation both in the corporate body and in the incorporated individual.[25]

While this formation might at first glance seem very far from a YouTube video or Insta caption, we can observe through the function of the cyber superego how individuals are governed and come to govern themselves via the structure of the network. In September 2011, Sean Duffy's conviction under Section 127 of the Communications Act 2003 and subsequent eighteen-week custodial sentence was the first high-profile conviction for trolling in the United Kingdom; Duffy pleaded guilty to posting messages on a Facebook memorial page dedicated to a young woman who had committed suicide.[26] It might at first appear that the conviction of trolling is an example of the cyber superego at play against the id; the usual formulation of an argument against social networking is that by conferring anonymity the device removes accountability and both allows and sanctions a permissive aggression that would not be countenanced in the face-to-face encounter. The troll, however, views their action as a corrective to homogeneity and a culture of conditioned social values. By posting content whose primary though latent purpose is to function as a representation of self-image, the social media user invites, in return, confirmation and affirmation of that image and of the ego, in the form of likes, reposts and so on. As the purpose of posting inheres in that reciprocity, we seek the response of followers and respond to it in kind by analyzing our metrics—what elicits the most likes?—then 'curating' future content accordingly. The response of the cyber superego thus trains the ego and models its future representations according to calculations of that recompense; the ego is disciplined to produce a self-image in line with prevailing mores and standards and, moreover, to internalize so as to be able to reproduce those standards iteratively. The cyber superego bears its collective pressure upon the individual and trains the ego to the extent that we act according to an awareness of its force at all times, on but also offline.

What distinguishes the cyber formation from its earlier incarnation in the Freudian cultural superego is its historical emergence from the information age and its socio-political situating within neoliberalism: where previously the superego conditioned the ego to be part of society, producing a concept of society by extension, the cyber superego evacuates the social even as it invokes it, ontologizing the Thatcherite worldview of a grouping of individuals through the transformative medium of the technological network. By utilizing individuals to bring other individuals into line according to how well they adhere to the dominant order and its values—self-capitalization; difference, insofar as it is permitted, leveraged as brand; competitive positioning—the cyber superego trains the ego not to be part of a society, responsible to the imperative of collective solidarity, but to be part of a contingent assemblage, wherein relation to self and to others is viewed in terms of self-investment and accrual. This habituation to live for others—meaning through their eyes, as human capital for oneself and for others, rather than in the service of a common good—turns the user towards an ontological self-disciplining while expunging the potential for radical thought or action, even though social media might ostensibly appear to provide a platform for such potential. The cyber superego, like the cultural superego, also operates to curb that which is aggressive, unacceptable or heterogeneous by bringing conduct into line with the market model. Politics is reconstituted by it as populist left and right-wing fringes, leaving an acceptable liberal democratic identity—in other words, the voice of 'common sense' that serves as the ideological branch of neoliberalism—to occupy the middle ground. As such, it works to elide radical difference, to allow sanctioned difference as a facet of diversity and, where possible, to assimilate movements with potential for such change to its rationale through its practices; we can consider here how various movements, from Occupy through Black Lives Matter to #MeToo, have been structurally incorporated through their networked existence. By training users to conform to consensus or forcing them to the margins of exclusion, the cyber superego cultivates a paradigm of self-constitution and interrelation in which the process of becoming human capital in late capitalist neoliberalism can be explicitly traced by analyzing its psychoanalytic dimension.

Capitalism and Desire

Mark Zuckerberg has come a long way in his self-professed mission to make Facebook a 'platform for all ideas'.[27] From its 2004 conception in a Harvard dorm room, Facebook went public in 2012 and has a current estimated worth of circa $600 billion. In the process it has colonized social media with the acquisitions of Snapchat, Messenger, Instagram and WhatsApp. The advance in use of social media has seen different platforms obtain to specific demographics: for example, Gen Z predominantly use Instagram, TikTok and to a lesser extent Facebook and Snapchat, while Facebook usage remains dominant in older demographics, as does Twitter, which has also found sub-foci such as Black Twitter, Academic Twitter and Political Twitter. The stratification of social media along generational lines is complicated by the communicative and linguistic cultures that platforms have engendered, as well as differing attitudes of belief or skepticism that pertain to reception of information and the understanding of what is represented by the platform itself. The latter rests on a prior perception of whether a platform is thought to be a new but neutral medium that occupies a space within an existing paradigm of vertical and hierarchical media, presuming the legal and ethical protections and standards of that model, or whether it is seen to be a component of a more profound change towards a horizontal, pluralistic information culture in which the proliferation of data, the ability of all users to be content creators and the openness to manipulation at individual and state level mean that the former paradigm is increasingly irrelevant and questions of objectivity fundamentally compromised. The problematic of advertising on social media receives significant legal and media attention, not least because legislative frameworks have not accounted for how adverts are utilized or misused on digital platforms. Debate in this area has coalesced around diverse but related issues: from non-declared Instagram-sponsored posts to targeted advertisements and their link to data mining, and most significantly, in 2019, to the role of Facebook in disseminating misinformation during election campaigns. This has centered around the refusal of Zuckerberg to institute a policy whereby Facebook would remove political advertising containing false information, on the grounds that do so would be against a corporate understanding of democracy and freedom of information. Ironically, this trades off the conflation of a distinction between old and new media paradigms that Zuckerberg has elsewhere been keen to dismantle: while social media in the Euro-American context theoretically gives everyone a voice, the reception of political advertising is still psychically governed by the presumed values of objectivity, authority and truth that adhered to its dissemination in mainstream media before the information revolution, compromised though those may have been. The residue of those values is formally exploited to create trust, while the content itself is false and/or incendiary but attains credence through the form, as it presents the continuation of an older conceptual model simply transposed to a new and transparent conduit.

Facebook has also routinely been the object of scandal, most recently around the Cambridge Analytica affair that resulted in Zuckerberg being called to Washington, DC, to account for its activities before Senate and House committee hearings. Although ostensibly concerned with the responsibilities of edge providers to user data privacy, the hearings exposed a number of latent tensions, including the perceptual gap between the actuality of the Facebook enterprise and the conceptual vocabularies that sought, and failed, to understand it through outdated twentieth-century paradigms located in the oil and banking industries. In both House and Senate the genesis myth of Facebook was a recurrent trope as a precursor to pro- or anti-regulation calls, according to whether the questioner viewed the platform as a monopoly to be centrally dissolved, or as a model of free entrepreneurship.[28] Zuckerberg himself drew on the founding mythos to turn the lexicon of disruption into one of modest contrition—'I think it's—it's pretty much impossible, I—I believe, to start a company in your dorm room and then grow it to be at the scale that we're at now without making some mistakes'.[29] When responding to questions on content policy by Chair Sen. Thune and Sen. Sullivan respectively, the birth of Facebook in the Harvard dorm was invoked by Zuckerberg to cast the enterprise as the millennial equivalent of a mom-and-pop operation:

> ZUCKERBERG [to Chair Sen. Thune]: [...] So, from the beginning of the company in 2004—I started in my dorm room; it was me and my roommate. We didn't have A.I. technology that could look at the content that people were sharing. So—so we basically had to enforce our content policies reactively.
>
> [...]
>
> ZUCKERBERG [to Senator Sullivan]: Senator, there are a number of important points in there. And I think it's clear that this is an area, content policy enforcement, that we need to do a lot better on over time.
>
> The history of how we got here is we started off in my dorm room with not a lot of resources and not having the A.I. technology to be able to proactively identify a lot of this stuff.[30]

Sullivan framed a variation on the theme that would become more pronounced in the next day's House Committee hearing: 'Mr. Zuckerberg, quite a story, right? Dorm room to the global behemoth that you guys are. Only in America, would you agree with that?'.[31] For Rep. Rush, Facebook was 'no longer the company that you started in your dorm room. Instead, it's one of—great American success stories'.[32] Framing Facebook's colonization of quotidian life, Chair Rep. Walden addressed its bedroom conception in his opening statement:

> WALDEN: You and your co-founders started a company in your dorm room that's grown to one—be one of the biggest and most successful businesses in the entire world.
>
> Through innovation and quintessentially American entrepreneurial spirit, Facebook and the tech companies that have flourished in Silicon Valley join the legacy of great American companies who built our nation, drove our economy forward, and created jobs and opportunity. And you did it all without having to ask permission from the federal government and with very little regulatory involvement.[33]

Walden then introduced the issue of monopoly by returning to the terms of Zuckerberg's own narrative:

> WALDEN: So you've mentioned several times that you started Facebook in your dorm room in 2004; 15 years, 2 billion users and several—unfortunately—breaches of trust later, Facebook's today—is Facebook today the same kind of company you started with a Harvard.edu email address?[34]

The origin story of Facebook thus serves a protean purpose, in that it functions to denote and facilitate multiple ideologies: at once the signifier of a millennial entrepreneurship; of a classic 1980s Reagonomic-Thatcherite capitalist ethos; of a dream of American exceptionalism realized; and of the tech start-up as incubator for accelerated corporate growth, 'grown [… but not] matured'.[35]

When she developed Foucault's model of *homo oeconomicus* to argue that neoliberalism, as the dominant order of contemporary reason, transforms every human activity and sphere of life, Brown revealed the extent to which, as both an invasion and an evacuation of the political by the economic, neoliberalism not only reconceives the values and principles of the democracy it purports to uphold but democracy itself, understood as the collective power to rule of the demos. Our case study is Facebook, around whose origins, rise and current market domination a constellation of issues coalesce; reading these through the prism of late Freud, we argue that the neoliberal revolution is not only incomplete without the tech revolution, but that technology is further expanding the ontological shift effected by it. That neoliberalism effects a usurpation of political categories through the language of governance and best practice can be seen in the transcripts of both the House and Senate hearings attended by Mark Zuckerberg, in which issues that are properly political are repeatedly elided by vocabularies of governance and practice, and a space or even possibility for political debate vacated. By stressing the operation of processes, the limits and extents of corporate duty and the procedures of reporting, the questions asked of Zuckerberg reveal the neoliberal logic predicating the debate even as they signal the failure to intervene in terms that would challenge that structural power. Indeed, Zuckerberg's answers deploy the same lexicon and occupy a shared ideological terrain. This obfuscates an examination of the relationships between Facebook, the self and the democratic polity, and recasts a political question—what is the nature of the platform and what is its power?—as a set of legal and procedural questions.

Mark Zuckerberg defines Facebook as 'an idealistic and optimistic company [...] focused on all of the good that connecting people can do'.[36] Along with Instagram, Facebook ostensibly functions as a network based on affective values *enabled* by technology, sharing and connection, rather than as a technology that modifies those values by metricizing them. In language calibrated to appeal to both the Republican and Democrat sides of the aisle, Zuckerberg carefully and repeatedly represented the social network as a *tool* rather than a matrix: '[a]nd, as Facebook has grown, people everywhere have gotten a powerful new tool for staying connected to the people they care about most, for making their voices heard and for building community and businesses'.[37] By mobilizing a vocabulary suggestive of the network's capability of facilitating the First Amendment right to free speech and expediting access to the free market, Zuckerberg de-emphasizes and diminishes both the power and implications of social media technology. By oscillating simultaneously between promoting its capacities and stressing its instrumentalism, he draws upon existing narratives that define social media technology as an enabling mechanism and an inherently neutral medium which, when used to benevolent ends, makes possible an expanded definition of society that aligns frictionlessly with the contemporary democratic imaginary. It is of course easy to contest this characterization as a variant of what is now termed conscientious capitalism. More profoundly, however, social media is not harnessing an already extant concept of society and, by extension, democracy, nor strengthening them, but fundamentally altering those concepts and their constitutive values even as it linguistically and semiotically encodes them as its postulates. Put simply, when social media is apparently promulgating society and democracy, its mechanisms are emptying them out and changing their meaning. Social network technology thus functions in a double space wherein it raises and relies upon the linguistic specter or after-effect of an already-evacuated political referent in an apparent defense of that democracy from attacks elsewhere, while being a key agent of neoliberalization.

Mark Zuckerberg presents his company as an example of a democratic network, akin to a Deleuzo-Guattarian rhizomic structure; as described in *A Thousand Plateaus* (1980), the rhizome is '[u]nlike a structure, which is defined by a set of points and positions', for it 'is made only of lines: lines of segmentarity and stratification as its dimensions, and the line of flight or deterritorialization as the maximum dimension after which the multiplicity undergoes metamorphosis, changes in nature'.[38] Michael Hardt and Antonio Negri explicitly discuss the shift in twentieth-century capitalism towards the post-modernization or informatization of production as one wherein 'the assembly line has been replaced by *the network* as the organizational model of production, transforming the forms of cooperation and communication within each productive site and among productive sites'.[39] By reimagining users as the nodal points on a vast, non-hierarchical, decentered network, the very structuration of the system has become celebrated as a return to democracy, but irony attends the fact that the deterritorializing effects of the technology have had the result of reterritorializing power and capital in Palo Alto. Network capitalism, reliant on the globalized immateriality of the market, has grown in parallel with and revived the remains of older forms predicated on land and commodities, which has led to conflict locally around rising house prices and gentrification in Californian communities, and globally in debates about tax avoidance, monopolies, precarious labor and the nexus between business, philanthropy and political influence. It is also notable that this has taken place against the backdrop of a post-millennial history of financial collapse, austerity and rising political populism. Deleuze and Guattari's schizoanalysis of free-market capitalism reveals it to be an organizational system that offers only a veneer of stability:[40]

> Underneath all reason lies delirium drift. Everything is rational in capitalism, except capital or capitalism itself. The stock market is certainly rational; one can understand it, study it, the capitalists know how to use it, and yet it is completely delirious, it's mad.[41]

This cycle of incessant recession is not the effect of a capitalism gone wrong, the fault of working-class subjects defaulting on sub-prime mortgages or investment bankers, but is an effect of the capitalist system itself.[42] The capitalists of the early twentieth century were engaged in an impossible fight to constrain the drive of society towards chaos. Deleuze refers to this 'schizo' dimension of the capitalist system and explains it through a chronology of desire: '[t]he true story [of capitalism] is the history of desire. A capitalist, or today's technocrat, does not desire in the same way as a slave merchant or official of the ancient Chinese empire would'.[43] The stellar rise in an era of financial chaos—crises are important to capitalism—of social media platforms such as Facebook and its acquisitions can be explained through their cultivating of individual desire and the manner in which that desire is then subsequently reinvested into the collective. To adopt another term from Deleuze and Guattari, who refer in *Anti-Oedipus* to the 'desiring machine' and its fundamental capacity to construct desire, Facebook recognizes and reorganizes subjects as desiring machines within an oligopolistic desire network.[44] In *A Thousand Plateaus*, the concept of the assemblage replaces that of the desiring machine. Desire is materially constituted through the assemblage, a concept of a social grouping open to alteration, reformation and intersection through other assemblages. The assemblage suggests that ontology is not fixed, but created from heterogeneous elements that form and re-form relations. 'All assemblages are assemblages of desire', and they function in tandem with the machine; in our case, a social machine and the network as assemblage:[45]

> It is the machine that is primary in relation to the technical element: not the technical machine, itself a collection of elements, but the social or collective machine, the machinic assemblage that determines what is a technical element at a given moment, what is its usage, extension, comprehension, etc.[46]

In the machinic assemblage of the desire network, it is the social aspect that is primary: the web of computers facilitating the network is the technical element determined by the social machine. Social networking operates on a model of desire as a process of perpetual production; in other words, desire is not acquired after the traumatic moment of fracturing or dissolution, but is, in contrast, extant from the very beginning of life. Deleuze and Guattari celebrate Freud for his discovery of the unconscious and then immediately criticize him for purging the unconscious of all radical alterity and for imposing upon it a classical symbology:

> The unconscious ceases to be what it is—a factory, a workshop—to become a theater, a scene and its staging. And not even an avant-garde theater, such as existed in Freud's day (Wedekind), but the classical theater, the classical order of representation. The psychoanalyst becomes a director for a private theater, rather than the engineer or mechanic who sets up units of production, and grapples with collective agents of production and antiproduction.[47]

The architectonics of Facebook reveal a more sophisticated and advanced understanding of the role desire plays in the contemporary capitalist moment. Zuckerberg understands intuitively that the unconscious is a factory, and social media technology an empire of desire production; Facebook does not face the threat of saturation in the market because it is driven by a desire that has no goal.

Users also reveal the hidden labor in the (net)work, as every click on the page, every minute spent on the site, every piece of data submitted can be liquidated and, in a strange perversion of Marx's theory of labor value, users are simultaneously the laborers and consumers. When they click onto their profiles and those of others, incessantly checking, incessantly updating, unable to resist just one more click, such apparent incontinence also represents an evolution of desire. How, though, is the motion towards refresh not merely another example—and an example *par excellence*, updated for the digital age—of repetition compulsion, ending in the Freudian schematic conclusion that all desire is predicated on lack?. In such an understanding, the itch to click becomes an attempt to fill the gap, repeated *ad infinitum*. We suggest that social media platforms present a mutation in desire according to two psychoanalytic schemas. The first is Freudian, specifically the understanding of desire as lack. These technologies represent an alternative ontology of desire, based upon this epistemological functioning of their interface with users. Effectively, users of Facebook, Instagram and so on are employing the platform as a visible structure which, crucially, is effaceable; in this mode social media technology doubles as a gateway to what we might call a desire network, a network that uses the platform as the prosthesis to access its circulation. In this understanding, each click functions not as a move towards a desired object, but as the access to, and pay-off of, desire itself. Pleasure is located in the process, rather than the visual object it leads to: the photograph, message, status update, online hook-up are by-products of the desire network. Social media plugs the subject into this network, and desire functions not upon a lack, opening up desire, nor towards a lack. With each click or tap onto Facebook or Instagram desire is produced, and each click or tap continues to produce desire: it becomes clear that such a repetition establishes a development in desire, where it is no longer the wish to access a picture, an update, a rumor—to access the specific *object* of desire—but desire itself that is the object, where the visual supplies merely a scaffolding. With social networks, the human subject is learning to take pleasure *in desire itself*: not in desire as a pleasurable by-product towards the object, nor even in the only place where it is conceded to be enjoyed as a primary drive, in lack, therefore as a masochistic pleasure. The pleasure—the pay-off—is the effect of desire; it is a learned pleasure, wherein the subject is educated to desire *desire* itself. For Deleuze and Guattari, '[a]ssemblages are passional, they are compositions of desire [...] there is not desire but assembling, assembled desire'.[48] Moreover, 'the rationality, the efficiency, of an assemblage does not exist without the passions the assemblage brings into play, without the desires that constitute it as much as it constitutes them'.[49] The assemblage is libidinal, and the way in which Deleuze and Guattari characterize the unconscious: 'the assemblage is fundamentally libidinal and unconscious. It is the unconscious in person'.[50] The network, if thought as an assemblage, is libidinal; if it, too, is constituted by desire, then the network is an assemblage that constitutes an altered desire and is constituted through that altered desire.

Facebook and Instagram develop the ontology of desire by making desire objectless, or rather, by making it an object to itself. In such a way, desire becomes its own network. Nor is this desire as understood in the sense of a Lacanian investment. Within that understanding, it is indeed conceded that desire is the primary goal of the subject, beyond the object in which it is apparently located. In the altered desire there is neither an undefinable lack, an abstract, that spurs the desire (the hope, say, that the next picture, the next update, will be the Platonic one) nor is it reached as the veiled real of the *objet petit a*. Rather, in this alteration desire is not towards any object. The object—the photo, the note, the update on the wall—becomes the *plus-de-jouir* of the desire network. It is not that there is an undefinable lack, an absence in the abstract, that spurs the desire; if anything, it is an excess. It is desire as objectless: the social network structure is merely the framework for a new psychic system installed through it. There is now a removal, though not an absence, of the specific object of desire. With the social network, the photos, the notes, the updates—the content of Facebook and also the site, the scaffolding of the social network itself—are no longer objects that mark the place and provide the material impetus for the liberation of desire (thus functioning as signifiers for the far more important operation they set in motion, which is a wholly psychic one) but are the *plus-de-jouir* of desire itself, already freed of material support, and of which this material effluence is the by-product. It follows, then, that neither are social media apps about chasing the platonic photo, party or connection but rather about the *process*, of which the visible end—the specific photo, party, connection—is not even a nominal object (which would imply the possibility of lack and thus re-enter into the Freudian schema) but the by-product of this altered modality of desire.

In *Anti-Oedipus* Deleuze and Guattari conceive their schizoid dream of a society wherein desire flows freely within the machine. For Deleuze and Guattari it is the desiring machines, in their multiple connections and dislocations, that break the tyranny of Oedipus, but it has been said that in doing so they discount its plurality; what could also be said is that Deleuze and Guattari still conceive of desire as being *towards* something or someone, towards an object. What we are suggesting is that in the development of desire we observe through social media technology, there is a difference from desire as configured by Deleuze and Guattari, and that ultimately this shift may better serve a depiction of contemporary society. We are proposing not multiple desires, or an excess, a constant production of desire that travels off in all directions of a network, but a network in which desire occupies the traditional space of subject and object. It effaces the requirement for a nominal object, and it is in the production of desire that the real is located. The subject experiences themselves *qua* subject in an altered way, no longer directing desire *towards*. It is, then, not production *towards* but production *of* which is the subject position, and where the subject locates the real. In effect the chronology has been altered: whereas previously production of desire could be the end of a process of production towards desire (even the ultimate end of the subject), what this developmental shift establishes is that there no longer need be a process towards desire. It is produced, without aim, and that is its aim. The material prosthesis—even where that prosthesis is in fact virtual—has been made completely irrelevant to both the beginning and the end of the process; 'content' is produced as waste. Such internalization means that desire now functions in its own circuit wherein no object of desire is more important than an understanding of the impetus and desire for desire itself. Desire is gratified, but gratified because it is yet always producing, never ending, because it is unending; the singular (specific) desire—the desiring *of* desire in that singular instance—is always towards the iterative, because general: the system is that of the desiring of desire, therefore the specific instance is always the general functioning of the system, rather than a devolved example of its abstract premise. This is not desire towards a lack but its satisfaction (though not the satisfaction of a lack). The structure of the social network removes the scaffold of the object and becomes instead the structuration of desire. Desire is not a closed system, but it no longer requires a specific object. The assemblage remains open by its nature, but we are asking what exterior, what machine, it opens onto: if the social machine, it has created the social in its image and effected, we are arguing, a change in its ontology. It remains open as an assemblage along lines of deterritorialization, but the mutation in desire, which constitutes the assemblage and by which the assemblage is constituted, effects a mutation in social subjectification and in capitalism. It is hard to see where resistance might effectively take place because the interior and exterior are interchangeable, and the relation the assemblage effects between desire and the subject in the process of subjectification ultimately strengthens the capitalist system. By appearing open, the network becomes a totalizing enclosure, not panoptic but self-regulating and self-sustaining. Both the machinic assemblage and late capitalism are mutating, reforming and reassembling along altered lines. Desire has progressed to function completely without even the fiction of a nominal exchange, a subject and object transfer in the traditional sense. It has been removed fully into the psychic realm.

And it is from that alteration of desire that the mutation of capitalism can be seen, for it is in the invisibility of desire (the removal of the object) that it may find its parallel. We suggest that it would be a capitalism wherein the fiction of its possibility as one among an ideological plurality is exploded. While capitalism functioned as it was traditionally systematized, as a financial system of monetary exchange in the form of hard currency for material goods, it shared its visibility as an ideology with the means of its conceptualization and was indivisible from them. As long as the support of capitalism is visible, it is prominent as a system and that prominence is a weakness: the visibility draws attention to its functioning, to its indivisibility from its means of functioning and to its status as an ideology. To draw attention to its status as an ideology is then to recognize the possibility of its existence *as* a possibility, among a plurality of others. What we here argue is that the removal of desire from the literal scaffolding of the external—and the concomitant mutation of desire into a network of production per se which it enables—also parallels the removal of capitalism into a wholly immaterial market system, where there is no requirement for the traditional support of capitalism, namely currency and goods. If through the assemblage desire mutates, so does the relationship between the subject and capitalism. In 'Postscript on the Societies of Control' (1992), Deleuze foresaw that the technological age would see a 'mutation in capitalism'.[51] Deleuze and Guattari were unable to determine the mutation; we are positing that it is effected in the network, and that in the concept of the social network the pre-vision of the information age takes place. This extends to technical machines, which are defined extrinsically in *A Thousand Plateaus*: through them, the state has 'substituted an increasingly powerful social subjection for machinic enslavement', subjecting the subject to the machine in a dynamic that redefines it and ultimately returns the society of control (defined against the society of discipline as one which exerts force through self-sustaining control mechanisms as opposed to disciplinary structure) to one of machinic enslavement.[52] For us, moving further into the tech era, the hardware or machine prosthesis gives way to a different kind of materiality constituted by the internet. It is correct to say that in this age, the increased subjectification returns us to a disciplinary enslavement and that the 'framework expands to all society [...] Social subjection proportions itself to the model of realization'.[53] In the functioning of the network is an assemblage unforeseen by Deleuze and Guattari, a framework which does not only expand to all society and expand proportionately and globally, but constitutes society in its mutated ontology. Imagined in abstract terms by Deleuze and Guattari, we suggest that the epoch of the social network within the information age constitutes the actual realization of those pronouncements.

Notes

1. Sigmund Freud, *Introductory Lectures on Psycho-Analysis*, in *The Standard Edition of the Complete Psychological Works of Sigmund Freud*, trans. by James Strachey, Vol. XVI (London: The Hogarth Press, 1963 [1917]), pp. 284–5.
2. Sigmund Freud, 'The Aetiology of Hysteria', in *The Standard Edition of the Complete Psychological Works of Sigmund Freud*, trans. by James Strachey, Vol. III (London: The Hogarth Press, 1962 [1896]), pp. 187–221 (192).
3. As an aside, the contemporary fetish within modern academia for archival studies and the fact that we are constantly reminded that we leave digital traces everywhere we click online, echo Freud's vision of mental life and physical life as being scaffolded upon a vast repository of memories.
4. Walter Benjamin, 'Excavation and Memory' *Selected Writings*, Vol. 2, Part 2 (1931–1934), "Ibizan Sequence", 1932, ed. by Michael William Jennings, Howard Eiland, and Gary Smith and trans. by Rodney Livingstone and others (Cambridge, MA and London: The Belknap Press of Harvard University Press, 2005), p. 576.
5. Ibid.
6. Sigmund Freud 'A Note Upon the "Mystic Writing Pad"', in *The Standard Edition of the Complete Psychological Works of Sigmund Freud*, trans. by James Strachey, Vol. XIX (London: The Hogarth Press, 1961a [1924]), pp. 227–32 (231).
7. This will be complicated further when Freud unleashes his theory of *todestrieb* (death drive) upon the psychoanalytic world with the later publication of *Beyond the Pleasure Principle.* For Freud, this human predilection towards destruction is an internal one that has existed for time immemorial.

8. Sigmund Freud, *The Ego and the Id*, in *The Standard Edition of the Complete Psychological Works of Sigmund Freud*, trans. by James Strachey, Vol. XIX (London: Hogarth Press, 1961b [1923]), pp. 3–63 (25).
9. David Harvey, *A Brief History of Neoliberalism* (Oxford: Oxford University Press, 2005), p. 3.
10. Brown (2015, pp. 35–6).
11. James Strachey, 'Editor's Introduction', *The Ego and the Id*, in *The Standard Edition of the Complete Psychological Works of Sigmund Freud*, trans. by James Strachey, Vol. XIX (London: Hogarth Press, 1961b), p. 7.
12. Freud (1961b, p. 27). Italics ours.
13. Freud (1961b, p. 36).
14. Freud (1961b, p. 34).
15. Freud (1961b, p. 25).
16. Freud (1961b, p. 37).
17. Sigmund Freud (1964b, p. 141).
18. 'Transcript of Mark Zuckerberg's Senate Hearing', *The Washington Post*, April 10 2018. N.p. Transcript courtesy of Bloomberg Government.
19. The Axios Event at which Parker made these comments was widely reported; see for example 'Ex-Facebook president Sean Parker: site made to exploit human "vulnerability"', *The Guardian*, November 9 2017 and 'Sean Parker: Facebook exploits vulnerability in human psychology', *cnet.com*, November 9 2017. These platforms remain largely free to users but that is not to say that they represent a form of benevolent social experiment on the part of their creators. Individuals including Sean Parker have discussed how the free-at-point-of-contact nature of these online platforms constituted a movement towards a new advertising model, whereby the attention of their users could be monetized through what has become known as attention economics.
20. Brown (2015, p. 33).
21. Brown (2015, p. 34).
22. Brown (2015, p. 34).
23. Freud (1964b, p. 145).
24. Freud (1964b, p. 134).
25. Brown (2015, p. 34).
26. 'Sean Duffy case highlights murky world of trolling', *BBC News*, September 13 2011.
27. 'Transcript of Mark Zuckerberg's Senate Hearing', *The Washington Post*, April 10 2018. N.p.
28. The Harvard dorm was invoked seven times in the Senate Hearing, five in the House Committee ('Transcript of Zuckerberg's appearance before House committee', *The Washington Post*, April 11 2018. N.p. Transcript courtesy of Bloomberg Government). It is worth noting that Facebook

began within the University and was designed in its first incarnation to connect students of select institutions, its attraction inhering in this initial exclusivity that then allowed it to grow virally.

29. 'Transcript of Mark Zuckerberg's Senate Hearing', *The Washington Post*, April 10 2018. N.p.
30. 'Transcript of Mark Zuckerberg's Senate Hearing', *The Washington Post*, April 10 2018. N.p.
31. 'Transcript of Mark Zuckerberg's Senate Hearing', *The Washington Post*, April 10 2018. N.p.
32. 'Transcript of Zuckerberg's appearance before House committee', *The Washington Post*, April 11 2018. N.p.
33. 'Transcript of Zuckerberg's appearance before House committee', *The Washington Post*, April 11 2018. N.p.
34. 'Transcript of Zuckerberg's appearance before House committee', *The Washington Post*, April 11 2018. N.p.
35. 'Transcript of Zuckerberg's appearance before House committee', *The Washington Post*, April 11 2018. N.p.
36. 'Transcript of Mark Zuckerberg's Senate Hearing', *The Washington Post*, April 10 2018. N.p.
37. 'Transcript of Mark Zuckerberg's Senate Hearing', *The Washington Post*, April 10 2018. N.p.
38. Gilles Deleuze and Félix Guattari, *A Thousand Plateaus: Capitalism and Schizophrenia*, trans. by Brian Massumi (Minneapolis, MN: University of Minnesota Press, 2004b [1980]),p. 21.
39. Michael Hardt and Antonio Negri, *Empire* (Cambridge, MA: Harvard University Press, 2001), p. 295.
40. We here retain the usage of 'schizo' when referring to Deleuze and Guattari's terminology, but place it within a historical theoretical context and emphasize that the term is redundant in modern clinical discourse.
41. Félix Guattari, 'Interview with Gilles Deleuze and Félix Guattari: "Capitalism: A Very Special Delirium"', in *Chaosophy: Texts and Interviews 1972–1977*, ed. by Sylvère Lotringer and trans. by David L. Sweet, Jarred Becker, and Taylor Adkins (Cambridge, MA and London: Semiotext(e)/ MIT Press, 2009), pp. 35–54 (36).
42. Faced with a saturation in the mortgage market in the United States, banks began to court constituencies that had been traditionally excluded from property ownership for the purpose of cultivating new markets and new profit streams.
43. Guattari (2009, p. 36).
44. See Gilles Deleuze and Félix Guattari (2004a: Chapter 1, pp. 1–57).
45. Gilles Deleuze and Félix Guattari (2004b, p. 441).
46. Deleuze and Guattari (2004b, p. 398).

47. Deleuze and Guattari (2004a, p. 62).
48. Deleuze and Guattari (2004b, p. 339).
49. Deleuze and Guattari (2004b, p. 339).
50. Deleuze and Guattari (2004b, p. 36).
51. Gilles Deleuze, 'Postscript on the Societies of Control', *October*, Vol. 59 (Winter, 1992), pp. 3–7 (6).
52. Deleuze and Guattari (2004b, p. 457).
53. Deleuze and Guattari (2004b, p. 457).

Works Cited

Wendy Brown, *Undoing the Demos: Neoliberalism's Stealth Revolution* (New York, NY: Zone Books, 2015).

Walter Benjamin, 'Excavation and Memory' *Selected Writings*, Vol. 2, Part 2 (1931–1934), "Ibizan Sequence", 1932, ed. by Michael William Jennings, Howard Eiland, and Gary Smith and trans. by Rodney Livingstone and others (Cambridge, MA and London: The Belknap Press of Harvard University Press, 2005).

Gilles Deleuze, 'Postscript on the Societies of Control', *October*, Vol. 59 (Winter, 1992).

Gilles Deleuze and Félix Guattari, *Anti-Oedipus: Capitalism and Schizophrenia*, trans. by Robert Hurley, Mark Seem, and Helen R. Lane (London: Continuum, 2004 [1972]).

Gilles Deleuze and Félix Guattari, *A Thousand Plateaus: Capitalism and Schizophrenia*, trans. by Brian Massumi (Minneapolis, MN: University of Minnesota Press, 2004 [1980]).

Sigmund Freud, 'The Aetiology of Hysteria', in *The Standard Edition of the Complete Psychological Works of Sigmund Freud*, trans. by James Strachey, Vol. III (London: The Hogarth Press, 1962 [1896]).

Sigmund Freud, *The Ego and the Id*, in *The Standard Edition of the Complete Psychological Works of Sigmund Freud*, trans. by James Strachey, Vol. XIX (London: Hogarth Press, 1961 [1923]).

Sigmund Freud 'A Note Upon the "Mystic Writing Pad"', in *The Standard Edition of the Complete Psychological Works of Sigmund Freud*, trans. by James Strachey, Vol. XIX (London: The Hogarth Press, 1961 [1924]).

Sigmund Freud, *Civilization and Its Discontents*, in *The Standard Edition of the Complete Psychological Works of Sigmund Freud*, trans. by James Strachey, Vol. XXI (London: Hogarth Press, 1964 [1930]).

Sigmund Freud, *Introductory Lectures on Psycho-Analysis*, in *The Standard Edition of the Complete Psychological Works of Sigmund Freud*, trans. by James Strachey, Vol. XVI (London: The Hogarth Press, 1963 [1917]).

Félix Guattari, 'Interview with Gilles Deleuze and Félix Guattari: "Capitalism: A Very Special Delirium"', in *Chaosophy: Texts and Interviews 1972–1977*, ed. by Sylvère Lotringer and trans. by David L. Sweet, Jarred Becker, and Taylor Adkins (Cambridge, MA and London: Semiotext(e)/MIT Press, 2009).

Michael Hardt and Antonio Negri, *Empire* (Cambridge, MA: Harvard University Press, 2001).

David Harvey, *A Brief History of Neoliberalism* (Oxford: Oxford University Press, 2005).

CHAPTER 4

Bodily Economies

> As far as the middle classes are concerned, the expense involved in psychoanalysis is excessive only in appearance. Quite apart from the fact that no comparison is possible between restored health and efficiency on the one hand and a moderate financial outlay on the other, when we add up the unceasing costs of nursing-homes and medical treatment and contrast them with the increase of efficiency and earning capacity which results from a successfully completed analysis, we are entitled to say that the patients have made a good bargain. Nothing in life is so expensive as illness—and stupidity.[1]

Self-Care and the Reality Principle

Moon Juice, Brain Dust, goop and smudge sticks: the recent trend towards 'wellness', a post-millennial, secular manifestation of that most LA of phenomena, the cult, revolves around the products, rituals and rhetoric of self-care. At the same time as the theory of late capital has turned towards considerations of precarious and affective labor, the two intersecting in considerations of care and of the body, the subject in capitalism has retreated to the sanctuary of a 'care' that is conceived as both protective and prophylactic, even as it renders the body subject and object of capital. This chapter asks how we might consider late capitalist constructions of care, particularly in thinking of care as labor and conversely, of the labor of self-care. It examines how leisure—the putative absence of work—becomes

M.-D. Dick, R. McLaughlan, *Late Capitalist Freud in Literary, Cultural, and Political Theory*,
https://doi.org/10.1007/978-3-030-47194-1_4

the site of labor and, via a late Freudian investigation in dialogue with Herbert Marcuse, considers how the body becomes the locus of the subject conceived as human capital. It suggests that we might think of wellness not as an 'epidemic'[2] but as a symptom, and analyzes self-care as both a practice and a language embodying a capitalist ontology with the body as its fulcrum. To 'work on oneself', to 'work out' and to engage in the 'work' of 'self-care': all are to conceptualize the body, at once indulged and placed under duress, as not only an object of aesthetics but a mode of capital, and a means of production.

In this chapter we question how we perform as human capital within contemporary history and conceive the body as an economy within which wider economies, both financial and psychic, intersect. The seemingly perpetual nature of capitalist democracy has imbued it with a sense of inevitability, and the perception of the inescapable nature of the late capitalist politico-financial system has witnessed the re-cathecting, in Freudian terms, of a radical spirit for change, away from the traditional institutions and apparatuses of power and towards individualized channels, such as that of the bodily image. Unable to improve society for the majority, twenty-first century subjects resort to strategies of physical and mental improvement (at one end of the continuum) and of physical and mental solace (at the other), based in the development of a lexicon that transfers the rhetoric of corporate markets to conceptions of personal wellbeing. The argument is underpinned by Freud's shift from a topographical to a structural schema of the unconscious, whereby he reworks the origins of ego development in *The Ego and the Id*. In this text Freud works out his psychodynamic theory to detail the ways in which external stimuli are psychically processed, conceiving of the 'body-ego' as the mental projection of the body surface.[3]

Self-care encompasses an at-first diverse continuum of activity: from sheet-mask Sunday, to the NHS Mindfulness website designed to teach the UK population techniques of mental health self-alleviation; from eating 'clean' to eating 'well', a class distinction that nonetheless belies underlying commonalities of attitude; from having a bath to having a glass of wine. It ranges from yoga before work, to therapy animals in the library. From going 'no-contact' with family members to weekend avocado toast or buying a daily latte, the latter one of those curious flashpoints that have taken on outsized significance as a sign of intergenerational communicative impasse: baby boomers exhort millennials to count up the cost of those coffees and invest instead in their future, while millennials point out that they have no such future in which to invest. Property ownership, stable employment and pensions being an irreality, the daily latte becomes a small salve in an otherwise relentless existence rather than an extravagance. Under the conditions of neoliberal late capitalism, the increasing attenuation of the self, and of the self as part of the *polis*, manifests in an increasing attention to the mind-body paradigm as signified in a multiplicity of such examples. What holds them together is their auto-reflexive quality: subjects engage in DIY practices of self-soothing designed not to sustain but to maintain, for the purposes of quotidian functioning within the workplace—which may be the imagined office of a laptop or a café table—and within the wider socio-political conditions of a world that feels inescapable.

As early as 2005, Wendy Brown identified self-care as fundamental to neoliberalism *qua* political rationality:

> neoliberalism normatively constructs and interpellates individuals as entrepreneurial actors in every sphere of life. It figures individuals as rational, calculating creatures whose moral autonomy is measured by their capacity for "self-care"—the ability to provide for their own needs and service their own ambitions.[4]

Since 2005 self-care has attained new significance in discourse, premised on this foundation but accruing different inferences and connotations. To explore the particular valences of the concept and its formation under contemporary capital, we turn first to Foucault, who traces the genealogy of the ethical subject to the practices of ancient Greece and Rome in *The Care of the Self* (1984), the third volume of *The History of Sexuality*, and in *The Hermeneutics of the Subject*, the series of lectures given in 1981–82 at the *Collège de France*.[5] Foucault outlines the ethical basis of the care of the self in the Socratic injunction to the pursuit of self-knowledge, where to care for oneself is to maintain a rigorous examination of one's own mind and behaviors through the exercise of philosophical inquiry, so as to attain a state of insight whereby the self reaches equilibrium in oneself and towards others. Foucault characterizes the ethical subject as one whose attention is turned dialectically upon the self, as constituted through various acts of self-inquiry and through ascetic living. The subject engaged in care of the self is thus the foundation of morality, because the exercise of attention has as its aim the pursuit of truth. *The Care of the Self* as both an ethics and a text starts with a discussion of dreams and of the centrality of dream work to its activity. Foucault begins with a seemingly Freudian echo, citing *The Interpretation of Dreams* as 'a manual for use in daily practice'; yet the book he references is not that of Freud but a second century A.D. treatise by Artemidorus, the remaining text of an ancient literature of oneiromancy that construes dreams as a sign from the future, rather than a map of the unconscious.[6] A certain futurity is built in to Foucault's argument, for example in his history of the ancients' move away from sexual freedom towards an increased moral rigor. In that this shift was not located in external legal proscriptions but in the turn towards the self, the attention to one's conduct, mind and body—and to bringing the self into discipline through such attention—constitutes a governance of desire by means of a strict moral contemplation that situates one in reflective relation to oneself. Foucault surmises that such scrupulousness has been linked to a growing emphasis on privacy, and to the emergence of 'individualism' that places the new focus on ethical rectitude within a diminution of the collective public democratic context; seen in this light, the exhortation towards self-reflection is attributed to the diminution of social bonds and the increasing atomization of society.[7] Foucault resists this reading, citing not only the continuing importance of civic life and interrelation within these societies but the centrality of the other to the activity of self-examination:

> it should be noted that the doctrines that were most attached to austerity of conduct—and the Stoics can be placed at the head of the list—were also those which insisted most on the need to fulfil one's obligations to mankind, to one's fellow-citizens, and to one's family, and which were quickest to denounce an attitude of laxity and self-satisfaction in practices of social withdrawal.[8]

Questioning the individualism 'so frequently invoked, in different epochs, to explain very different phenomena', he distinguishes between the figure of the independent individual, the realm of private and domestic life and the relation to self as an object of knowledge and action for the purpose of attainment of moral truth.[9] Foucault dismisses individualism as the cause of the new sexual privation, instead locating it in the historical rise of the cultivation of the self, a concentration on self-relation characterized by the principle of care of the self. The care of the self is a work of scrutiny through which one seeks self-possession; it is understood as part of a philosophical inquiry and towards philosophical ends, the art of living that teaches one how to die. Constituted as a 'true social practice', it both depends on others and is for others.[10]

In the same way, psychoanalysis represents a turning inwards that brings mind, body and conduct under examination in order to situate the self in relation to itself and to others. A post-Cartesian inquiry, it reframes attention to the care of the self away from morality and towards psychology, seeking to bring the patient to insight via a dialectical relation to the analyst; like the care of the self of antiquity, its aim is to resolve psychosomatic disturbance through self-inquiry and to examine the self in its relation to others. To appeal to his bourgeois constituency, Freud emphasized the intensely practical aspect of analysis; as the epigraph to this chapter makes clear, he framed the expense of analysis as a means of speculating to accumulate, playing off short-term cost against the long-term savings on continued treatments and nursing homes. In his economic costing there also lies a premonitory tremor of the logic of neoliberalism that builds the bridge between care of the self and self-care, when Freud determines that patients will have made a 'good bargain' when one takes into account the 'increase of efficiency and earning capacity which results from a successfully completed analysis'.[11] Freud's address to the middle classes anticipates the language and logic of the futures contract, where the bourgeois client is encouraged to 'go long' by investing in themselves as a means to securitize greater economic prosperity. Yet it would be mistaken to derive from the pages of 'Papers on Technique' an image of psychoanalysis as a solipsistic endeavor; indeed, Freud is clear in the opening epigraph to this chapter that its outcome serves civilization, and the analytic experience more broadly requires a communal dynamic. The stage setting and directions of Freudian psychoanalysis may visually establish analysis as centered narcissistically upon the patient but, as Freud reminds in several of his later works, the drama of an analysis takes place between two actors and a playbill of unseen ghosts from history. Two years before his death, Freud published a paper that would prove to be one of his last interventions into the field of psychoanalytic theory and in which he stresses the communality of the analytical experience: the self-knowledge of the patient requires the expertise and presence of the analyst/neighbor figure to elicit it. In 'Constructions in Analysis', Freud attends to a misperception that the analytical turn inwards towards the unconscious of the analysand represents a retreat into egocentrism. Freud reminds any student of psychoanalysis of what he considers to be a 'fundamental fact', that every analysis involves 'two people, to each of whom a distinct task is assigned'.[12] The analyst is tasked with the responsibility to 'make out what has been forgotten' or repressed by the patient, and to '*construct*' or reconstruct from the traces of information given an understanding of the patient's unconscious life and, by extension, the reason that they have decided to financially invest in psychoanalysis.[13] Julia Kristeva reads the communality of psychoanalysis in humanist terms throughout her study of foreignness and otherness in *Strangers to Ourselves* (1988). Kristeva reimagines the analytic process via a universal humanism that undermines notions of psychoanalysis as a narcissistic enterprise: '[t]the foreigner is within me, hence we are all foreigners. If I am a foreigner there are no foreigners'.[14] Not only is the unconscious a foreign territory, but any exploration of it requires the presence of the Other; further, any recognition of the ultimate foreignness of the psyche must render strangers no longer foreign. The radicalism of psychoanalysis, for Kristeva, derives from a schematizing of individuals as fundamentally estranged from themselves, and the principle that an understanding of self is only possible through the intervention of an external, foreign, agent. Psychoanalysis is reworked by Kristeva as 'a journey into the strangeness of the other and of oneself', a collective process that produces 'an ethics of respect for the irreconcilable'.[15]

When tracing the conceptual shift from care of the self to self-care, the emphasis on communality diminishes as the Freudian emphasis on productivity increases. What is the significance of self-care in the contemporary moment, and what is its relation to the body?. One of the ways in which we can view the late capitalist body and its relation to the self is through how it is constructed by and reflected in the discourse and practices of attention. We can thus begin to consider how the subjectivity of *homo oeconomicus* is formed via the body and its significance for understanding the subject of late capitalism and the functioning of ideology through that subject. The semiotics of self-care have supple relations and dimensions, which we group here under three broad areas. What is central to all is a relation to productivity and to work: in each we can discern how the turning inward of attention reflects and reproduces the internalized market logic of neoliberalism that transforms *homo oeconomicus* into the subject of human capital.

The first category is ameliorative and can be identified in a range of activities and commodities signifying warmth, plenty and nurturing: box-set binges, nights on the sofa, an array of blankets and throws, sensory security. It manifests in soft and luxurious versions of leisure clothes, designed for imaginary first classes, or in adult onesies; in weighted comforters, pillows designed to cocoon the body from the world, in ASMR, and in the transformation of our personal space for the gaze of others. This mode of sanctioned retreat configures rest as recovery: less nesting than escape, less an act of nurturing than one of nursing, it is an insulation and recuperation that functions through literal protective mechanisms which form a barrier to the world while being presented as indulgences. Here, there are two seemingly contradictory impulses. One acknowledges the vulnerability of the body under capitalism, rather than its resilience. In this way, it represents capitalism as all-encompassing and without alternative, rather than as that which can be resisted, and self-care becomes a form of generating the 'resilience' required to survive within the system. There is also within this mode a distinct relation to commodity capital, as it becomes another outlet for conspicuous consumption even where there is an apparent total eschewal: for example in concerns around material ecologies, environmentalism and zero waste, now effectively harnessed by capital and with undeniable class dimensions. Self-care is an embodied relation to neoliberal rationality and to the capital that underpins it; the irony lies in its sadomasochistic aspect, where the receiver, having internalized the logic of exploitation, is also the exploiter of the body. In this cycle of lavish punishment, the subject is identified with production to the extent that it is not merely indivisible from but determinative of being; that self-care pretends to annexe or create a safe space is an acknowledgment that one can no longer opt out of capitalism. Practices of attention further enable this shift by facilitating its move to the body which has become increasingly abstracted in the age of the cognitariat, reorienting capitalism to the corporeal and providing for its reproduction through incorporation; it gains access to the body as a site of investment and as substrate, under the pretense of alleviating the psychic and somatic effects of late capitalism. By performing self-care upon our bodies we partake in a privatized act that is also an act of self-privation and make ourselves the locus of reproduction.

The second category is that of maintenance, in which there is an effort towards consideration and balance, of seeking to achieve equilibrium of mind and body in order to remain operational in the world. Here, we most often see the invocation of work-life balance as a term, and it involves time-bound and purposeful activity, with strong ideological subtexts of improvement, renewal and sustenance: competitive or at least regular running, reliance on tracking apps, gym-going, Pilates and a variety of atavistic spiritual practices for a secular age, yoga, T'ai chi, reiki and so on. The emphasis is on routine, incorporation and rational order; these activities are part of a lifestyle of efficiency and are typically practiced before or between work, during a notional lunch-hour or prior to an evening commute. They are part of a broader commitment to a *considered* life, whether framed as maximized or measured and deliberate: one of globalized localities, authenticity, against the backdrop of sustainability. An update on the old dictum *Mens sana in corpore sano*, there are also class or class-aspirational aspects to this method of self-governance. Self-care becomes a program of maintenance rather than sustenance, one of careful meting and individualized renewal; there is a solipsistic dimension to its apparent concern with the subject in its relation to the world, in that those relations are ordered through self-care as economies of energy expenditure and personal reserves. As a marketing tool and as a trend, it is commonly indexed to wellness and an imaginary constellated around the natural: plant-based, palo santo, guided meditation, exercise (which both takes the place of religion and achieves a spiritual dimension in itself), hashtagged and curated aesthetics that level out alterity and reduce difference to marketable traits. If self-care has a palette, it also has an affect, one that is about optimizing time as much as optimizing the self: there is *no rest* for the virtuous.

The third, related, category we characterize as optimizing. In it, we might include the derided—and therefore most-publicized—reaches of the phenomenon: jade eggs, alkaline water, sound baths and myriad other ways of granting monetized access to the ostensibly natural in the goal of 'reconnecting' the self to the self. These extreme examples are unhelpful in so far as they weaponize gender and falsely sequester self-care as an object of analytical inquiry for feminist debates. As they overlap with the wellness lifestyle trend, they also promote the conflation of wellness with self-care and serve the purpose of deflecting, through a reduction to the absurd, a serious scrutiny of a pervasive, widespread and nuanced shift in conduct. Within this category, however, there is a continuum of examples. Among them, we might consider the draw towards the 'raw' and the 'clean'—'clean' eating, raw states, whether of food, or emotion (e.g., in the trend towards discussion of vulnerability), or the trend for skin, the bare, makeup-less face that reveals the hyperregimen of care from within and without. No matter the degree to which these are actually carried out, their prevalence within our cultural landscape is indicative of the impetus towards optimization seen in this type of self-care, in other words to perceiving the self as capital in which one must invest in order to maximize return; self-care puts the responsibility back onto the individual to cultivate and improve their assets. Such conspicuous forms are interesting in that they appear to divert from consumer capitalism and on to the self returned to ethico-spiritual values but, in fact, represent the move from that stage of capitalism to late capitalist economization. Critics focus on cost, waste and solipsism—which are exorbitant—but these are not the most radical aspect: such 'care' is a hybrid, where the visible consumption is a vehicle or adjunct to the conversion of human capital within the market paradigm, as it presumes to reinvest it through self-care in ostensibly non-capitalized forms of 'growth' of self.

The purpose of this analysis is not simply to denigrate such practices but to make them visible as such, and in a particular way. By lifting the veil on how seemingly disparate cultural and daily practices might be analyzed as a connected matrix of coping strategies, we propose that they are not merely effects of neoliberalism but a mechanism for its ontological reproduction. All three categories share a strong ritualistic component, and common to them is that the performance of self-care shows an awareness of the pressure of living within the neoliberal system, in that it is constituted as a reaction to those pressures. All, too, can be read as modes in which the human capital paradigm of selfhood that Wendy Brown has demonstrated as emergent from the free-marketization and metricization of non-economic spheres is displayed, internalized and reproduced.

To understand how this takes place, we turn to the relationship between self-care and work. Precarity manifests not only in the obvious places—zero hours contracts, the gig economy—but also in the casualization of highly educated workers, in the metricization of established professions along outdated business models and among the so-called entrepreneurs of virtual economies. The contemporary concept of work is that of an all-encompassing environment, or more accurately is all-encompassing as our environment: constant economic anxiety, the dissolution and extension of the 9–5 day, over-work indexed to KPIs and the exhortation to personal 'branding', engendering constant vigilance and activity over said brand, all converge to situate the subject always within a virtual workspace. More obvious drives towards productivity, such as the tech-industry pioneered transmutation of workplaces into home and play environments through the supply of free food, leisure perks and other benefits designed to maximize time in the office, are in fact cruder manifestations of a universal reorienting of relation to working life. In such a way, self-care becomes a sanctioned removal within, rather than from, that space: alleviation is revealed to be its secondary or supplemental function, while its primary design is to condition us to the system. Whether protection, maintenance or optimization, all aspects of self-care share what is an essentially recuperative function. Across all categories the underlying causality of the symptom of self-care is exposed by the tension in its discourses between prevention and protection, luxury and necessity. It replicates class relations in one body which is at once the agent and receiver, subject and object, of that activity. Consequently, it also casts us in a position to ourselves that is as detached as it is intimate, reified through the gaze of the other, branding oneself and turning the body simultaneously into the site of labor and site of economy. This logic draws together phenomena that are subtle and obscure along with those that are more explicit, from academic profiles to YouTube vlogs. Where before we might have internalized class relations via their visible socio-economic structuration, we now internalize those relations and reproduce the microsphere in ourselves, overseeing the transformation of our bodies into content. The rationale of self-care is predicated on the body for capital and as capital, a resource to be fed upon, cannibalized and groomed under the guise of nurture and preservation. The body becomes a way to flaunt our relation to capital, as well as a place of flagellation demonstrating multiple manifestations of being under capital, in capital and constructed as human capital.

At the beginning of *Civilization and its Discontents*, Freud approaches the functions of the pleasure principle and reality principle through a discussion of happiness, which takes the form of the deferral of suffering. He designates 'techniques of living' for the procurement of this aim in light of his supposition that unhappiness comes from three sources: the forces of the external world; imposed social regulation by others; and our body, derived from nature, which we experience as a traitor to us in its long decline.[16] Among these techniques Freud identifies as examples intoxication through artificial stimulants; the deliberate denial of the instincts, one example of which is 'prescribed in the worldly wisdom of the East, and found in Yoga'; and the displacement of the libido and derivation of pleasure from 'psychical and intellectual work'.[17] The latter he admits as imperfect because it is open only to those of particular talent and 'habitually fails when the source of suffering is one's own body'.[18] Freud appends an extended footnote to this statement:

> When there is no special dispensation in a person which imperatively prescribes what direction his interests in life shall take, the ordinary professional work that is open to everyone can play the part assigned to it by Voltaire's wise advice [p. 75 above]. It is not possible, within the limits of a short survey, to discuss adequately the significance of work for the economics of the libido. No other technique for the conduct of life attaches the individual so firmly to reality as laying emphasis on work; for his work at least gives him a secure place in a portion of reality, in the human community [...] Professional activity is a source of special satisfaction if it is a freely chosen one—if, that is to say, by means of sublimation, it makes possible the use of existing inclinations, of persisting or constitutionally reinforced instinctual impulses. And yet, as a path to happiness, work is not highly prized by men. They do not strive after it as they do after other possibilities of satisfaction. The great majority of people only work under the stress of necessity, and this natural human aversion to work raises most difficult social problems.[19]

The footnote is significant in several respects. First, as it relegates to the margins a subject that Freud himself confesses is key to understanding the theory of the libido; the tension is evident in the excursus, which points to an unease that the importance of work has not been fully explored and that its economic function has itself been dealt with too economically. The footnote then makes a crucial intervention into the theory of the reality principle when Freud declares that work constitutes the principal attachment between the subject and civilization. Its placement within the theory as a mechanism for displacing libido, along with the suggestions that it forms a social utility to the working of civilization and in the dispensation of existing inclinations, implies a bourgeois identification with work as career, rather than as labor for wages, that poses an issue for an accommodation of its role within the late theory. Freud indicates an anxiety over the nature and significance of work within the wider scope of his thought when acknowledging that what he deems to be its qualities do not recommend it to people, seemingly resolving that dilemma in the attribution of a 'natural' aversion of people to work, rather than in the structural causation which the admission that a 'great majority of people only work under the stress of necessity' might point towards. Though work is literally relegated to a footnote in *Civilization and its Discontents*, that decision points tacitly towards its importance to the whole. In the present period, we might add the practice of self-care to the list of techniques of living designed to alleviate suffering. Its focus on the mind and body, together with its ostensibly protective purpose, places it within the remit of the categories listed by Freud. Self-care claims to place attention on the body and mind for the purposes of improvement but we might consider how, despite its apparent function, it operates instead as a means of bringing the body into line with the dictates of civilization, and specifically to the regulations of work as they now order social life more broadly. In this way, self-care would cease to serve as a technique for living, or more accurately would appear to do so while in actuality performing in the service of the reality principle.

In *Eros and Civilization* (1955) Herbert Marcuse develops Freud's thesis on the reality principle, one of his central claims being that repression as it functions through the reality principle is exercised in the post-Fordist era through over-development of production, a commitment to productivity, and the internalization of the rationality on which it depends. Mass democracy is the political system through which the reality principle is introjected, and this 'democratic introjection of the masters into their subjects' becomes the mechanism that reproduces the system and precludes liberation or the possibility of revolt.[20] By leveraging the productivity of that society as it is enabled by technology, it makes its subjects agents of their own suppression, allowing those who control the system to operate within the illusion of freedom it bestows and to make the masses complicit in 'voluntary servitude'.[21] Marcuse not only locates this complicity in the colonization of culture by the machine of political and corporate interests, but also identifies the over-development of productive forces as the instrument enabling it. His diagnosis appears as a mid-century heralding of the reach of neoliberalism, a term Marcuse does not employ but whose contemporary dawning in retrospect suffuses his text; present-day reading can figure the neoliberal political rationality outlined by Brown as an outgrowth of that identified by Marcuse, which draws on Freud's theory of cultural repression as it is internalized under the conditions of twentieth-century commodity capitalism.

Under what Marcuse terms the rule of the 'performance principle', identified as the historical form of the reality principle, subordination to society progressively develops to a maturity that is 'impersonal, objective, universal, and also increasingly rational, effective, productive'.[22] Domination is implemented through the division of labor relations such that '[s]ociety emerges as a lasting and expanding system of useful performances; the hierarchy of functions and relations assumes the form of objective reason: law and order are identical with the life of society itself'.[23] His hypothesis that a civilization of plenty would defend itself against the 'specter of a world which could be free' by turning productivity against its citizens and making of it an instrument of control has proven correct, as has his observation that the movement of social control into the 'formerly free regions of consciousness and leisure' has provided for the advance of the reality principle into the domain of the pleasure principle, obscuring subordination to its demands under 'spurious liberties, choices and individualities'.[24] Yet, writing in the mid-twentieth century, Marcuse could not have foreseen the ends to which the alignment of domination with social labor would extend, with its concomitant effects of rationalizing further domination and preventing revolt. The transfer of control from an individual to a system has been so totalizing that the relation of leisure is in multiple ways completely bound to that of work, as an index of subordination to the governing ideology or reality principle. Marcuse foreshadows Brown when he warns that the conflation of liberty and repression 'permeates all spheres of life the world over. The rationality of progress heightens the irrationality of its organization and direction'.[25] If the violence of the system now inheres in the internalization and replication of a political rationality that extends into all aspects of life, it has also progressed from the capitalism of the assembly line and office that are identified by Marcuse as sites of alienated labor and entered beyond them into the home. In this formation, the home becomes a locus of labor as a place of work and is further converted from a place of leisure to one where work is extended precisely through that leisure. As such, Marcuse's expectation that alienation and the elimination from labor of the human element could create the conditions whereby human beings might ultimately go beyond the performance principle and be liberated from labor seems now a utopian aspiration. Marcuse proposes the possibility that with totally alienated labor—a movement towards full automation—would come an opportunity to free being into 'the sphere outside labor which defines freedom and fulfilment, and it is the definition of the human existence in terms of this sphere which constitutes the negation of the performance principle'.[26] Instead, our alienation from our labor has resulted in the total colonization of the concept of productivity, parallel to a loss in visibility of labor conditions. The core neoliberal values to which it is harnessed have been able to infiltrate arenas heretofore closed to their reach and import economization into their domain, strengthening the overarching reality principle and resulting in an ontological alienation.

Marcuse was writing at a historical juncture where affluence, gauged to technologized productivity, was the new condition of society. His conception of the repressive state, however, remains one that is visible in its material effects: a constellation of references based in commodity capitalism, and the wielding of systemic power in warfare at home and abroad, particularly in the colonies, as a physical manifestation of technological and scientific domination. This emphasis on materiality extends to his theory on the body as a possible site of revolt, whether in the field of guerrilla warfare or in the sphere of sexuality, where he proposed it could be liberated from labor into the domain of Eros, or pleasure; the body was a potential site for the resistance, 'revolt as a matter of physical and mental hygiene'.[27] What we have seen instead, as we have moved from commodity to market capital, is the liberation of the system from material to immaterial realms and the subsequent unharnessed drive to productivity. Marcuse's optimism that technology would lead to a higher development of society, wherein over-production could be phased out and with it the psychological and bodily effects determined by its rationality, has been not only proven false but routed by technology itself, in that it has both instrumentally enabled and conceptually modelled the move to a 24/7 productive society. What self-care achieves is the subordination of the pleasure principle to the reality principle *even in* the delimited disbursement of that pleasure that already falls within the confines of the reality principle. The potential threat of the body to the system has not been realized, as the system has succeeded in co-opting and disciplining the body to its repression, making it an instrument rather than merely a site of effects. Because the body offered the potential to resist the system due to its relation to production, it is significant that it has been brought in line in that area where the rupture might have been most at risk of occurring, that of leisure, or its putative freedom from productive repression.

Marcuse's contention that progress would depend on 'the opportunity to activate repressed or arrested *organic*, biological needs: to make the human body an instrument of pleasure rather than labour' could not anticipate the ways in which the body would, in the absence of industrial labor, be appropriated to the financial market and itself reimagined as a material embodiment of its forces. *Eros and Civilization* asks, still hypothetically, '[c]an we speak of a juncture between the erotic and political dimension?'.[28] In the twenty-first century the body has shifted from being the obstacle to oppression to become its key locale, aligning the sensible to the political in ways that entrench the current system and foreclose other political responses. Self-care appears as a total refutation of the pleasure principle and a complete deference to productivity under the guise of the minimal recompensation of pleasure. As a practice, self-care figures the neoliberal body in dialectic with austerity and production: for example, in intensive exercise or bodily regimens that present as a new kind of affluence signified by asceticism or minimalism. This we might call the privation of affluence, whereas, in another manifestation, the cocooning instinct (seen for example in the trend towards Scandinavian *hygge*) presents as another form of response to austerity and to the demands of productivity. The reality principle as it has developed under neoliberalism, and as it is realized in the instruments of neoliberal governmentality, has elevated productivity to a matter of physical and mental hygiene, so that Marcuse's liberatory site has not only not come to pass but has been sublimated by the system to the codes of work. Society has not been able to reject affluent productivity and open the space to new ways of being, but has hyper-accelerated productivity while dispensing with affluence—or, to be more correct, reserving it to the minority. One manifestation of this acceleration is the civilizing of the body to the reality principle via a technique that manages to subordinate the pleasure principle to the overarching purpose of regulation. Self-care assumes the purpose of a palliative care, in parallel with what is revealed ultimately as a superego function of discipline. Rather than preventing or mitigating suffering from the twin sources of the external world and the body, self-care is a further form of suffering visited upon the body it pretends to alleviate. It constitutes an iterative means by which the reality principle brings the body under its directives, conditioning it to ideology and functioning as an apparatus of that ideology in the act of appearing to appease it.

The Work of Self-Care

On first glance, we may not see common ground between social media affirmations, obesity guidelines and the 'cancelling' of so-called toxic individuals. All of these examples are however consciously framed as self-care, from which we can see how the imperative towards auto-nurturance takes dispersed and seemingly unconnected forms. That the discourse is being used in this way might at first seem a tangential instance of language pervasion, but analysis of the practices gathered diversely under its term lays bare commonalities underlying its effects. Some of the illustrations outlined above are not, on the face of it, like the other: while some are affiliated directly to individualized hyperconsumerism, others engage the rhetoric for ostensible reasons of public health, specifically to target crises predominantly among socio-economically disenfranchized citizens. The former present as part of a considered routine that amounts to a secular ritualization, with connotations of intellectualism and of optimization. They represent a careful calibration of the meting out and recuperation of energies, economic and deliberative, that vaunts the neoliberal version of the life well-lived: its reduction to productivity in all areas. They are also self-generated, whereas the latter tend towards didactic regimens of mental and physical activity or avoidance, externally imposed and disseminated through institutions of the state and public governance. These are designed to mitigate or prevent pathology via self-triage, obscuring not only the removal and underfunding of professional services but more importantly the socio-political causation of those effects, a point to which we will return for development later in this section. One of the ways that this nuance of class iniquity within self-care is made manifest is in its relationship to time, which is central to the practice whether it is conceptualized as recharging, sustaining, investing in oneself, taking time out (from working life) or as gaining time (by correcting habits deemed bad, in other words those that cause economic strain on services). The tension in neoliberalism over what constitutes the time of work is directly indexed to the understanding of what work is; where work used to have a time and a place, the relation between the worker and their labor was most visible and along with it the relations of class and politics to the subject. While this began to erode after the post-Fordist era and in the period of deindustrialization, the success of the current economic paradigm has been in turning work from a labor to a market model and obscuring these visible relations. That work no longer has a distinct time or a necessarily fixed place means that our understanding of our work—and for whom it is done—becomes obscured, making the externally imposed market model easier to internalize. Leading on from that primary internalization, the transference of the market model across all areas of our life, including those which, as Brown points out, have previously been exempt, is seamless. The ontologization of the market within the subject is more difficult to effect when our relation to work is clear, which is why metricization is key to neoliberalism. Brown's contention that the subject is made complicit in becoming human capital through the extension of the metric model into heretofore non-economic spheres can be mapped out in what we consider a now-crucial element within the wider scope of self-care, that of leisure time.

Leisure time is vital to this sociological and ontological shift precisely because it has traditionally been the one sphere where the worker was free of direct labor relations and, consequent to that, the sphere in which the freedom of subjectivity could at least ostensibly be asserted. As the place and time where work was not, it allowed for work to be seen as such (the hire of labor for wage) and defined the subject as one whose primary relation was to their autonomy and interrelation with others. Leisure is key to the success of turning the labor model into the market model because incursion into this space represents the colonization of one subject position by another, beginning with the myth of the 'career' which sold the teleological fallacy of personal progression so that the worker became auto-invested in their own exploitation; we might think here of the now-ironic invocation of 'work-life balance' as an offshoot to understanding how the ideology of careerism serves the interests of neoliberalism by encroaching 'work life' upon 'life' so that the distinction begins to collapse. Late capitalism has seen the virtual disappearance of the career model, which has now given way to the 'portfolio career' and to increasing precarity in the remaining professions: short or fixed term contracts, notional contract hours to extort overproduction and metricized KPIs. Alongside these the gig and virtual economies have grown, making hot desks of coffee shops and living rooms, turning hobbies into ventures and monetizing private lives. The current discourse of agility is integral to the reproduction of that logic: terms such as 'disruption', 'pivoting', 'data fluency' and 'responsiveness to change' belong to a lexicon that marks its users within the ideological position they propagate even as it inures them to it. The adoption of this communal language first empties out then repoliticizes that language to ulterior ends; here, we could cite the current vogue for 'collectivity', 'ecologies', 'sustainability', 'collaboration' and 'creative economies', evidence of an appropriation of commonality to serve radically individuated ends. By virtue of its very technocracy it makes the grounds of objection difficult to articulate, since any resistance is framed as a disproportionate attack on common sense. We might also think of the broader co-opting of diversity to corporate agendae, as evidenced by practices of greenwashing and brownwashing that serve as public relations exercises rather than commitments to transformative equality and diversity policy. Self-care joins this vocabulary as another term that has historically both represented and acted as a force in the evolution of this ontological change, and it actively constructs the economization of the sphere of leisure in ways that are multiple and far-reaching. It represents the conquest of the economization model as it has extended into the furthest reaches of our private life, the ones that, most importantly, provided for alternative modes of being predicated upon ontological relations to the self and to others that rested on community, interrelation and removal from work.

One of the most basic ways in which this takeover has been effected is that when we are overworked, leisure becomes a response to work: it has a recuperative rather than restful function and is a reaction that places work psychically at the center as the organizing principle of our free time. That in turn recasts leisure for the purposes of work and free time as time *off* from work; on another level, leisure time becomes an escape from work between the closure and beginning of working hours. This is complicated in the contemporary era, first as the inducement to productivity in all areas has seen a blurring of work time into 'free' time, through the joint encroachments of technology and overwork that have led to the dissipation of the latter not only literally but also conceptually: there is potentially never a time when we could not be working. The recasting of precarity as opportunity turns us from workers into own-brand entrepreneurs, monetizing free time and totalizing all time as work time. So we are encouraged to build our brands, not in the hope of thriving but of surviving. Into this comes self-care, the perfect expression of the neoliberal colonization of time in which leisure is only permissible if productive. Even more than work time, leisure time is crucial to neoliberal ontologization. Previously the one sphere where the worker was free, leisure time played a central role in maintaining the visibility of capital relations *qua* the rent of labor. As the free market collapsed the rigidity of the working day, leisure, its activities and the relations they involved, remained a potential pressure point of resistance and needed to be converted to market ends to alleviate that risk. When the neoliberal model takes over, leisure ceases to exist conceptually and instead becomes variously a vehicle to suppress breakdown or to continue the hyperindividualizing of the self through regimes of attention. In both of these it goes beyond a response to work and itself becomes a kind of work; most crucially, it is perceived as such, so that the body becomes a site of labor in and of itself. Under this paradigm our bodies exist insofar as they are bodies for work and must be looked after for that work, but they also exist paradoxically as bodies traumatized by work, stressed by work (this is the default option), which it is our responsibility to look after in order to neutralize its effects under the guise of care and so to keep going. Figuring the body as both a sanctuary and a resource, self-care does not merely prepare and revitalize the working body, nor does it simply offer a displaced haven for the mind, but instead obviates the concept of the body at rest. The neoliberal body is a body at once divorced from labor and never absent capital.

Marx's chains of bondage are heavy and become more so when we try to alleviate them in forms that draw us further in, neoliberal logic literally incorporating the transfer of agency for its reproduction to the individual through the performance of leisure time. When the self becomes work itself, the colonization of the metric model—measurable, evidenced, maximized—diminishes moral, ethical and political dimensions and interrelations. Capitalizing (on) ourselves, work becomes internalized through the action of both the ego and superego. Individuated and atomized, workers function as a constellation of embodied micro-corporations of one. The consequences of this ideological takeover are evident: erosion of workers' rights becomes easier to effect; unemployment is individualized rather than being a collective issue or seen in its social context; and from complying with our conversion from economic actors into market subjects, we move to ourselves effecting that shift. Self-care optimizes the subject for the market, dissolving the self-relation and scrutiny that are proper to care of the self ***and*** an exercise of those values attained through it, free of the market, that would allow for a resistance. Ironically, it is through the activity of leisure rather than that of work that the logic of neoliberalism achieves totalization, succeeding where the more visible practices of the workplace might fail, reproducing and embodying the market within us. In such a way, neoliberalism circumvents the problem of leisure by legitimizing it through the ideology of the free market: leisure properly conceived is no longer permissible, and there is no free time. Living life has been edged out to the margins to the extent that practicing basic tasks and looking after oneself have been refigured reflexively as self-care. Daily activities that were previously separated from work are co-opted into its sphere via the mantra of productivity and are also recast as luxuries and modes of indulgence that accommodate and make space for more work: for example, having dinner as a family or with friends, having a lunch break, taking a walk, taking a break from the internet, exercise, having a past-time. We do not cut down on work or retreat from its logic, we move it into another scene and legitimize its monopolization. This is also why any analysis that views self-care as merely a response to neoliberalism can only be partial, since it is part of neoliberal ideology and reproduces it. More than the way capital induces us to tend the body for work—two weeks' holiday, seven hours' sleep, regular breaks—self-care is also the way capital co-opts the body for its ideology, enabling it to become more pervasive, the terms of resistance less clear. Even this construction of leisure as making space for work fails to fully account for what is happening, which is that life itself is becoming reconfigured as self-care: anything that was previously outside of one's working life is condensed and becomes a moment of self-conscious 'opting-out', meaning that which was not made capital or was outside of its direct ambit, is re-modelled as self-care and brought within the rationale of productivity.

We have been arguing so far that self-care is a conduct and conceptual vocabulary that amounts to a case study through which the process of the neoliberal economization of all spheres of life can be demonstrably viewed and understood; however, it is also an emergent sign from the future in which the class dimensions of neoliberal ideology can be identified. In so far as free-market economics purportedly offers the means to abolish class through the ethic of hard work, the truth of its enmeshment in traditional class structure can be concealed. On a macro level, the acquisition of wealth is guaranteed by the exploitation of the working and non-working poor, whether directly or indirectly (e.g., through the avoidance of fair taxation). On a micro level, the drive to acquire financial status is explicitly framed as the supervening of hereditary circumstance. Margaret Thatcher knew that the key to the free-market economy, the economic base of neoliberal ideology, was responsibilization: her infamous claim to 'back the workers, not the shirkers' epitomizes the transfer of risk from the social collective to the individual. In this speech delivered to the Young Conservative Conference in 1975, Thatcher expanded on the fallacy that individual agency could overcome structural power in determining life chances:

> I believe we should judge people on merit and not on background. I believe the person who is prepared to work hardest should get the greatest rewards and keep them after tax (*applause*).
>
> That we should back the workers and not the shirkers (*applause*): that it is not only permissible but praiseworthy to want to benefit your own family by your own efforts (*much applause*). Liberty must never be confused with license, and you cannot have liberty without a just law impartially administered (*applause*). You would not have political liberty for long if all power and property went to the State (*great applause*). Those who prosper themselves have a duty and responsibility to care for others, and I believe individual responsibility does not stop at home, but extends to the community of which we are all a part.[29]

Thatcher's recourse to community anticipated her later declaration that there is 'no such thing as society', returned to in David Cameron's vision of a 'Big Society' that divested state functions to localized voluntary networks.[30] Initiatives designed to tackle a societal epidemic of depression and loneliness, from community allotments to The Chatty Café Scheme (the corporate partner of which is Costa Coffee in the United Kingdom, owned by Coca-Cola), transfer the responsibility of the care of citizens from the state and devolve it to the level of the individual. The post-Thatcherite concept of a collective is that of responsibilized individuals, whose success or failure is due to their ability to prosper, or not, under their own efforts. By putting the emphasis on the individual, such logic removes society as the *a priori* unit in relation to which we see ourselves, and with it also elides the ability to see structural and systemic forces of inequality that operate on the wider scale of class demographic, whether these are defined by wealth or traditional divisions. The effect of neoliberal encroachment in the United Kingdom, seen first in the displacement of state functions to the private sphere, was to remove the social apparatus of care at a governmental level and by virtue of doing so, to atomize and destabilize the concept of society. As a lever for responsibilization, self-care occupies an instrumental function within this framework alongside another non-synonymous but related term, resilience. Hypostases of neoliberal ideology, both might be used to consider the fundamental tensions that give rise to and are hidden in them.

There has been a recent boom in journalism parsing the politics of self-care, most of which covers the same territory: the evidenced rise in the term on Google Trends as a response to the current political climate, a citation of Foucault and an attempt to reclaim the practice for marginalized communities in our contemporary epoch by situating it, via Audre Lorde, as a historical act of political resistance.[31] In scholarship, critics have also identified self-care as an index of the contemporary socio-economic and political landscape, analyzing how it privatizes responsibility, obscures the structural causes of environmental stress and depoliticizes the subject. Inna Michaeli proposes that it might be recuperated from neoliberalism through a framework based in feminist criticism and as a practice for collective care, bypassing its current construction.[32] This argument is part of a wider school of thought (see, e.g., Sara Ahmed, who is cited in Michaeli's work and widely within this debate) that interrelates BAME, LGBTQ+ and feminist concerns to recover self-care as a political act. Such work seeks to reclaim self-care by charting its genesis from medical discourse to

Lorde and the Black Panther movement, which appropriated the term for minorities to describe their autonomous provision of care in lieu of the failure of state healthcare systems and extended it to encompass protective and self-sufficient action under repressive political structures.[33] The reformulation of self-care as a means of resisting the system is however problematic, in that it is difficult to set it apart from and conceive of it as resistant to capital (even in a weakened form of caring for oneself under capital), where the concept is produced from, implicated in and reproductive of the contemporary regime. It suggests that the current paradigm of self-care is one version among possible alternatives, rather than a concept overlaid by and now indivisible from its contemporary historical construction. The term is contaminated by the structure to which it is tied, regenerating the system with each citation, whether verbal or physical. The connection between mental health, resilience and self-care has been argued by Francis Russell, the latter as a form of self-management reproducing neoliberal governmentality in order to shore up the psyche disordered by capitalism, its conditions and crises.[34] Drawing on Foucault and Silvia Federici, Russell proposes that self-care be made visible as a new form in which capital exploits and depoliticizes the subject but maintains that we might still have recourse to the practice, by viewing it as a form of reproductive labor and thus 'negotiating the ambivalence of self-care' through the emancipatory politics of Federici.[35] He locates this ambivalence in the paradox of self-care as a contemporary practice that entraps but one that has historically been relied upon by minorities:

> for a great number of marginalized people, self-care is not simply the only form of care available, but is can [*sic*] also be understood as an act of defiance against a hostile state or structure—e.g., patriarchy, white supremacism, or heteronormativity. For this reason, it is vital that the tension internal to self-care is maintained, and that its emphasis on individualism and resilience is not given precedence over its necessity.[36]

The premise that self-care can presently be used in such a way is contestable except to explain necessity in terms of a survivalist strategy, since the distinction is that self-care does not just preserve us to take more of the system, or to mitigate its effects, but now conditions us to the system itself. This disciplinary function means that its ability to represent a political act is now compromised under the era of finance capital. If we return to 'care of the self', that terminology reintroduces a political dimension that must always be lacking from current definitions of self-care, which are born of neoliberalism and cannot be conceptually divorced from the reproduction of its logic. One feature that self-care makes visible, as a by-product, is the purpose of reproductive labor and its value to capital: that is the traditional role of the woman in preparing the man and children for work, and increasing their productivity. It does so not as a resistance to capital but as a further individuation: in doing so however it points to the exhaustion of neoliberalism where, under new and ever more attenuated labor conditions, extending to all walks of life, traditional social formations can no longer either serve those conditions or be maintained by them. Instead of 'wages for self-care', the eponymous title of Russell's article that echoes Federici's argument in favor of 'wages for care', we are living in an era of self-care for wages, where the self does not exist in the Marxian sense *for* capital, but *as* capital and subsumed to it.[37]

It is important for this rationality to rethink care, because care in its traditional form prohibits the ability to individualize; it is a profoundly social behavior, one which, as Federici has argued, is indivisible from social reproduction but which also forms a resistance to capitalism. Late capitalist work divides us from the bodies of our mothers, from the company of our peers and from our selves. Self-care thus takes the form of a *pharmakon*, at once the cure for this division and the poison that cements it by virtue of disciplining our bodies and minds to free-market economics and the individualism that derives from it. Through metricization, we are conditioned to the economic model of the subject; through self-care and other discourses, that policy of responsibilization is effected and internalized, with the body as the substrate enabling ontological incorporation of neoliberalism. Self-care conceptually enables the erosion of social care—by which we mean, on an ethical level, care within a wider socius and care for that socius, and, on a governmental and public policy level, universal care provided within a state framework. It inures citizens to inequality on a personal and a structural level by disciplining us to accept these conditions, and shifts the blame for not doing so onto a failure of resilience. By deploying the terminology of agility—self-reliance, resilience, adaptability—it counsels that we should be able to cope and thrive in environments of austerity: food banks; growing crises of public health and homelessness;

casualization; falling real term wages; anti-Union laws; and the privatization of public services.

While the educated subject is expected to proactively become the agent of their own self-care, the state intervenes to train the masses; central to this endeavor is the reification of basic human needs as self-care, which recasts the fundamental as supplemental. Cooking at home, sleeping, speaking to friends, seeing family, rather than being the norm, are now represented as variously part of a regime, as a pleasure, or as a necessity to further enable production. Where practiced as a kind of protectionism, it is an admittance of the totalization of the system. What passes for hedonism now would have previously been seen as banal domesticity, and even such luxury has to have a dividend, whether in its function as a sign of care, or in health benefit, or in online sharing; which latter, from clicktivism to Instagram posts, institutes a memetic reiteration that makes it one of the only sanctuaries in which commonality, if not solidarity, can now be found. Instead of asking what is wrong with the structure, we accept this mutation of life into an optional extra in which we can partake to alleviate the stress of our environments. This can take several forms: one is a public health discourse that is silent about the correlation of the effects of economic and political policy on mental and physical wellbeing, but advocates self-control and reflexive care as part of its management. Here, care takes the form of what was previously a given: eating well, exercise, social interaction. Another is the valorization of the regime, wherein life is scheduled as part of a routine: diarized 'me' time, regular coffee breaks, 'date night'. Such conditioning diminishes legal rights—to leisure, to family life, to protection of working life—and rebrands social relations, rights and responsibilities as optional, individualized and bespoke. Corporate wellness agendae are design features of the neoliberal institution to permit further exploitation of workers: by providing resilience workshops, group knitting and therapy animals, they place the onus on the worker to ameliorate the effects of their environment while allowing health services to continue under-resourced and overarching structures to remain unchallenged.

The discourses from which these activities flow then attribute growing inequality to the inability to *take care* of oneself as a means of justifying ever-more savage public and private policy. Self-care is effectively reflexive governance in line with prevailing political ideologies: it replaces the function of care, which allows us recourse to values outwith that ideology, and removes the capacity to resist it. If care of the self entails reflection on our conduct, designed for the good of others and our own capacity to exercise free will within that social body, here we see the removal of the reflective dimension and its replacement with the reflexive, conveyed in repeated activity that literally embodies and internalizes this refashioning of subjectivity. In and through it, the social underpinning of community is removed as the inward turn cedes to the turn inward of self-care. We can see clearly here a concrete example of how the reality principle of post-millennial neoliberalism transforms a political subject into human capital: one in whom politics is incorporated as they are turned into an agent of transnational global economic ideology, while simultaneously losing the capacity to act as a citizen and as part of a communal society. The purpose of care of the self is to attain freedom of mind to perceive conditions objectively; it demands custodianship of the self for others. The conditions required to mount a resistance to neoliberal logic and the everyday practices of management that are predicated upon it at both a global and local level assume a subject whose self-perception is aligned with care of the self, rather than self-care. Solidarity requires subjective autonomy and agency, not individualism, which is why it is here, in the battle for two paradigms of subjectivity signified in the difference of these terms, that the problematic is visible.

Notes

1. Freud (1958, p. 133).
2. Cf. Amy Larocca, 'The Wellness Epidemic', *New York* Magazine, 26 June 2017.
3. After Freud's death Lacan returned to the ego-ideal, as the basis for his reworking of it as the *imago* that features during the Imaginary stage of infant development. Lacan goes beyond Freud in strengthening the determining role that the body plays in the formation of the ego-ideal and constructs the Imaginary as centered upon a moment in which the body directly shapes an individual's psychological development. The infant subject who, according to Lacan, experiences their subjectivity as a fragmented body, unable to exert control over their limbs, mistakes the reflected image they are confronted with during *le stade du miroir* as an image of bodily unity. The infant subject's sense of disunity compels them to misrecognize the Other as an image of perfection, the legacy of which will haunt the Lacanian subject for the rest of their lives. For Lacan, the psychic phenomenon of the Ideal-I, this Other version of ourselves with which we are always striving to reconnect, and which prompts us to go travelling in order to 'find' ourselves or to embark upon expensive wellness therapies in

order to be the 'best' version of ourselves, is conceived as a moment of bodily misrecognition (*méconnaissance*). See Jacques Lacan, 'The Mirror Stage as Formative of the *I* Function as Revealed in Psychoanalytic Experience', in *Écrits*, trans. by Bruce Fink (New York, NY: W.W. Norton & Company, 2002 [1966]), pp. 75–81.

4. Wendy Brown, 'Neoliberalism and the End of Liberal Democracy', in *Edgework: Critical Essays on Knowledge and Politics* (Princeton, NJ and Oxford: Princeton University Press, 2005), pp. 37–59 (42).
5. Michel Foucault, *The Care of the Self, The History of Sexuality* Vol. 3, trans. by Robert Hurley (London and New York, NY: Penguin, 1990 [1984]); Michel Foucault, *The Hermeneutics of the Subject: Lectures at the Collège de France 1981–1982*, ed. by Frédéric Gros and trans. by Graham Burchell (New York, NY: Palgrave Macmillan, 2005).
6. Foucault (1990, p. 4).
7. Foucault (1990, pp. 41–2).
8. Foucault (1990, p. 42).
9. Foucault (1990, p. 42).
10. Foucault (1990, p. 51).
11. Freud (1958, p. 133).
12. Sigmund Freud, 'Constructions in Analysis', in *The Standard Edition of the Complete Psychological Works of Sigmund Freud*, trans. by James Strachey, Vol XXIII (London: Hogarth Press, 1964h [1937]), pp. 255–69 (258).
13. Freud (1964h, pp. 258–9).
14. Julia Kristeva, *Strangers to Ourselves*, trans. by Leon S. Roudiez (New York, NY: Columbia University Press, 1991 [1988]), p. 192.
15. Kristeva (1991, p. 182).
16. Freud (1964b, p. 77).
17. Freud (1964b, p. 79).
18. Freud (1964b, p. 80).
19. Freud (1964b, p. 80), footnote 1.
20. Herbert Marcuse, 'Political Preface 1966', in *Eros and Civilization: A Philosophical Inquiry into Freud, with a New Preface by the Author* (Boston, MA: Beacon Press, 1966 [1955]), xi–xxv (xv).
21. Marcuse (1966, xiii).
22. Marcuse (1966, p. 89).
23. Marcuse (1966, p. 89).
24. See Marcuse (1966, pp. 93, 94; and 100).
25. Marcuse (1966, p. 101).
26. Marcuse (1966, pp. 156–7).
27. Marcuse (1966, xvii).
28. Marcuse (1966, xv and xxi).

29. 'Speech at Young Conservative Conference' February 8 1975, in *Observer*, February 9 1975, margaretthatcher.org.
30. Interview for *Woman's Own*, September 23 1987, margaretthatcher.org.
31. See Ester Bloom, 'How "Treat Yourself" Became a Capitalist Command', *The Atlantic*, November 19 2015; Laurie Penny, 'Life-Hacks of the Poor and Aimless', *The Baffler*, July 8 2016; Marisa Meltzer, 'Soak, Steam, Spritz: It's All Self-Care', *The New York Times*, December 10 2016; Arwa Mahdawi, 'Generation treat yo'self: the problem with "self-care"', *The Guardian*, January 12 2017; Jordan Kisner, 'The Politics of Conspicuous Displays of Self-Care', *The New Yorker*, March 14 2017; Aisha Harris, 'A History of Self Care', *Slate*, April 5 2017.
32. Inna Michaeli, 'Self-Care: An Act of Political Warfare or a Neoliberal Trap?', in *Development*, September 2017, Vol. 60, 1–2, pp. 50–6.
33. See Sara Ahmed, 'Selfcare as Warfare', feministkilljoys.com, August 25 2014.
34. Francis Russell, 'Wages for Self-Care: Mental Illness and Reproductive Labour', in *Cultural Studies Review*, Vol. 24, No. 2, September 2018, 26–38.
35. Russell (2018, p. 35).
36. Russell (2018, p. 35).
37. On wages for care, see Silvia Federici, *Revolution at Point Zero: Housework, Reproduction, and Feminist Struggle* (Oakland, CA: PM Press, 2012).

Works Cited

Wendy Brown, 'Neoliberalism and the End of Liberal Democracy', in *Edgework: Critical Essays on Knowledge and Politics* (Princeton, NJ and Oxford: Princeton University Press, 2005).

Silvia Federici, *Revolution at Point Zero: Housework, Reproduction, and Feminist Struggle* (Oakland, CA: PM Press, 2012).

Sigmund Freud, 'On Beginning the Treatment: Further Recommendations on the Technique of Psychoanalysis', in *The Standard Edition of the Complete Psychological Works of Sigmund Freud,* trans. by James Strachey, Vol. XII (London: Hogarth Press, 1958 [1913]).

Sigmund Freud, *Civilization and Its Discontents*, in *The Standard Edition of the Complete Psychological Works of Sigmund Freud*, trans. by James Strachey, Vol. XXI (London: Hogarth Press, 1964 [1930]).

Sigmund Freud, 'Constructions in Analysis', in *The Standard Edition of the Complete Psychological Works of Sigmund Freud*, trans. by James Strachey, Vol XXIII (London: Hogarth Press, 1964 [1937]).

Michel Foucault, *The Care of the Self, The History of Sexuality* Vol. 3, trans. by Robert Hurley (London and New York, NY: Penguin History, 1990 [1984]).

Michel Foucault, *The Hermeneutics of the Subject: Lectures at the Collège de France 1981-1982*, ed. by Frédéric Gros and trans. by Graham Burchell (New York, NY: Palgrave Macmillan, 2005).
Julia Kristeva, *Strangers to Ourselves*, trans. by Leon S. Roudiez (New York, NY: Columbia University Press, 1991 [1988]).
Jacques Lacan, 'The Mirror Stage as Formative of the *I* Function as Revealed in Psychoanalytic Experience', in *Écrits*, trans. by Bruce Fink (New York, NY: W.W. Norton & Company, 2002 [1966]).
Herbert Marcuse, *Eros and Civilization: A Philosophical Inquiry into Freud, with a New Preface by the Author* (Boston, MA: Beacon Press, 1966 [1955]).
Inna Michaeli, 'Self-Care: An Act of Political Warfare or a Neoliberal Trap?', in *Development*, September 2017, Vol. 60, 1-2.
Francis Russell, 'Wages for Self-Care: Mental Illness and Reproductive Labour', in *Cultural Studies Review*, Vol. 24, No. 2, September 2018.

CHAPTER 5

Culture in the Age of Death Drive

Kultur and Cultural Production

When, at the end of *Civilization and its Discontents*, Freud writes that 'we may expect that one day someone will venture to embark upon a pathology of cultural communities', he marks the end of a decisive movement that takes place across the body of his late work away from the analysis of the individual and towards an analysis of culture.[1] In order to further situate this arc in relation to our contemporary moment, we begin this chapter with a discussion of Freud's definition of *kultur* and its relationship to cultural production. In section two, we examine the fate of Freudian psychoanalysis within the discipline and consider how its legacy was compromised by the formative reception of psychoanalysis as 'a work of culture', institutionalizing its purpose as a process of alignment to the dictates of civilization. Our final section develops these dual understandings of culture to consider contemporary production in late capital and its illumination of the architecture of restriction upon the individual, in light of Freud's theorizing of death drive.

At the beginning of *The Future of an Illusion*, Freud makes a pronouncement on an ambiguity, present throughout his late work, that centers upon his use of the word *kultur*; he writes that 'I scorn to distinguish between culture and civilization'.[2] In his accompanying introduction, Strachey includes a note that outlines the choices made by the translator when negotiating any potential ambiguity, but does so in a way that stays

M.-D. Dick, R. McLaughlan, *Late Capitalist Freud in Literary, Cultural, and Political Theory*,
https://doi.org/10.1007/978-3-030-47194-1_5

true to Freud's supposed failure or reluctance to discriminate conceptually: 'it seems unnecessary to embark on the tiresome problem of the proper translation of the German word "*Kultur*". We have usually, but not invariably, chosen "civilization" for the noun and "cultural" for the adjective'.[3] Strachey's attempts to offer editorial precision immediately fade as he introduces another source of uncertainty by way of the qualifier 'usually, [...] not invariably'. Here we learn that both Freud and Strachey set out to employ 'culture' and 'civilization' in such a way that any distinction is semantic and not conceptual.

Freud may refuse to explicitly acknowledge the difference between culture and civilization, but throughout his late work he mobilizes different understandings of culture in singular and precise ways, moving between the cultural unit, analogous to civilization, and a narrower sphere of cultural activity. The debate surrounding Freud's use of ***kultur*** has been extensively staged, but in *Civilization and its Discontents*—his most concentrated psychoanalytic investigation into the relationship between the individual and the structured reality that they inhabit—Freud touches upon the distinction between culture as it is conceived more broadly and in the narrower sense of material achievement. Freud's refusal to 'distinguish between culture and civilization' is made apparent in the economic equation that underpins the findings presented throughout this late text: the greater the civilization, the more discontent we become. Indeed, *Civilization and its Discontents* sets out the role of culture in curbing the individual's desires for total satisfaction of pleasure, which would otherwise result in unrestrained aggression towards others and the inability to function communally. This prohibition on gratification operates through the exertion of the reality principle on the pleasure principle, such that individuals accept a diminished and delayed pay-off of pleasure in return for the recompense of the security of communal living, which also entails a protection from the drives of other individuals. Throughout *Civilization and its Discontents* Freud celebrates human mastery over the natural world as evidence of the sovereignty of humankind, arguing that civilization is a means to safeguard ourselves not only from the violence of the natural world, but also from the threat of violence from others in our Hobbesian state of nature. Clearly under the anthropological sway of figures such as James George Frazer at this point, Freud establishes the psycho-anthropological origin myth of communal life as one predicated on the sacrificing of genital love. This inhibited aim, as Freud would term it, represents a psychoanalytic primal moment wherein we are led to forfeit the demands of our drives in the service of the reality principle, thus accepting a degree of daily suffering in return for delayed gratification and the safety of community.

Within this equation Freud distinguishes between culture as a synonym for civilization and the output of that cultural unit, which might be designated itself as culture in the narrower sense, that which is produced to reflect the ideals of the civilization and to uphold them through its consumption. Although art and aesthetics are central to Freud's practice and feature throughout his body of work in writings on Shakespeare, Jensen, da Vinci, Michelangelo, Dostoevsky and Poe, among others, it is here that he ventures to consider the specific importance of art within the economy of culture, as he alludes to it in one of the later definitions of 'civilization' within the text:

> We shall therefore content ourselves with saying once more that the word 'civilization' describes the whole sum of the achievements and the regulations which distinguish our lives from those of our animal ancestors and which serve two purposes—namely to protect men against nature and to adjust their mutual relations.[4]

Civilization is comprised both of repressive frameworks (laws, social mores, prohibitions) and achievements that offer a narcissistic reflection of a culture's values, chief among which is its artistic output. Art occupies a special place within culture for both the artist and the consumer. For the former, it offers a sublimation of the instincts and displacement of libido through the joy of creation. Such satisfactions seem 'finer and higher', though they remain problematic as they can be experienced by only a select few.[5] For the rest, Freud situates the importance of cultural production in three ways: the first is its role in allowing a modified form of the psychic insulation from the external world that is felt by the artist when he retreats into his inner processes. Freud theorizes that this might be shared by the masses through the satisfaction of illusions, which are of a special category in that, arising from the inner life of the imagination, they are recognized as such but in a manner that the 'discrepancy between them and reality' does not intervene in their enjoyment.[6] First among these 'satisfactions through phantasy' is the enjoyment of the work of art, 'an enjoyment which, by the agency of the artist, is made accessible even to those who are not creative';[7] although Freud notes that though art offers an inestimable value of pleasure and consolation to those who enjoy it, it remains a substitute pleasure or 'mild narcosis' that can bring about only momentary relief and cannot compensate for real suffering.[8] The aesthetic production of a cultural unit occupies another important function in stabilizing and reproducing that civilization, as a form of psychic patrimony that guarantees it and forms part of 'its assets in the shape of ideals and artistic creations', offering a pay-off in satisfaction that pacifies the pleasure principle and maintains the cultural unit.[9] This is where Freud again implies the importance of cultural production to the upholding of civilization as an economy of shared but non-altruistic interests: while it would seem given that the ideals of a culture 'determine achievements', he suggests instead that its achievements first determine its ideals, which are constructed from the output—a combination of internal talent and circumstance—in a process of narcissistic mirroring, the subsequent output proceeding then to perpetuate and strengthen those ideals.[10] The suppressed classes participate in this patrimony of shared ideals, which can only be fully enjoyed by those in power, by taking pride in their culture as it is defined in those values against others, thus in turn preventing revolt by allowing identification with the ruling class and by seeing its cultural ideal reflected in them. Artworks present an issue here, since they offer 'a different kind of satisfaction' to the cultural unit and remain the preserve of the ruling class, as the masses are subject to the strictures of work and lack of access to education.

Yet Freud must incorporate the work of art to his theory because of the primacy it has been afforded within the class of achievements, a primacy that he first attempts to ground in its conceptual standing as a paradigm of substitutive satisfaction:

> As we discovered long since, art offers substitutive satisfactions for the oldest and still most deeply felt cultural renunciations, and for that reason it serves as nothing else does to reconcile a man to the sacrifices he has made on behalf of civilization.[11]

Moreover, it functions as an instrument fortifying commonality through shared aesthetic experience and by strengthening a constructed value set through the cultural achievements it depicts.[12] Freud accommodates the importance of cultural production to civilization by pointing to the requirement of the cultural unit to seek something higher once it has attained its base goal of mastery over nature, that marker of civilization that sees 'people directing their care too to what has no practical value whatever, to what is useless', in other words to beauty, which must be revered in nature and recreated in artistic achievement.[13] Alongside cleanliness and order, beauty occupies 'a special place among the requirements of civilization'.[14] Here, Freud seeks to justify his *fin de siècle* sentiments by hypothesizing that if the characteristic of civilization is its elevation of 'man's higher mental activities—his intellectual, scientific and artistic achievements—and the leading role that it assigns to ideas in human life', the importance of these lies in their satisfaction of human needs as motivated by the dual goals of utility and pleasure pay-off.[15] If culture and civilization have a shared conceptual basis as the achievements and apparatuses that structure the constrained life of the individual in society, there is a form of culture within that wider repressive framework that possesses an important superstructural function of concealing and mediating the full repression that modern subjects enter into, or to which they are subject.

It is at the beginning of the fifth chapter of *Civilization and its Discontents* that Freud introduces into his social-anthropological theory of civilization the great discovery of his late writing: the principle of *todestrieb* or death drive. Alongside the principle of Eros, Freud theorizes that the death instinct possesses a disruptive ability to pull all organic and, in the case of civilization, inorganic, life towards destruction. It exerts an incessant pressure upon society—'civilized society is perpetually threatened with disintegration'—such that society requires inoculation against *todestrieb* not only by means of a perpetual sacrificing of individual aggressiveness, but by the deployment of a fourth psychic force, distinct from the individual, that Freud terms the cultural superego.[16] The desire to live together, as expressed via the re-cathecting of sexual love dispersed across the socius, proves insufficient as a means of binding communities of people together in a stable way. As we have shown in chapter two, stability required the election of a Freudian elite which understood the psychic reality of individuals as desiring subjects and was able to implement ideas, policies, commandments and injunctions at government level to check base impulses:

> Civilization has to use its utmost efforts in order to set limits to man's aggressive instincts and to hold the manifestations of them in check by psychical reaction-formations. Hence, therefore, the use of methods intended to incite people into identifications and aim-inhibited relationships of love, hence the restriction upon sexual life, and hence too the ideal's commandment to love one's neighbour as oneself—a commandment which is really justified by the fact that nothing else runs so strongly counter to the original nature of man.[17]

In the paragraph that follows, Freud shifts focus to critique what he considers to be the fundamental principle of Marxist philosophy: the designation of private property as the root cause of all social inequity. Freud remarks that 'I have no concern with any economic criticisms of the communist system', but remains assured that 'the psychological premises on which the system is based are an untenable illusion'.[18] Freud dismisses Marxist theory as utopian in so far as he holds it to be predicated upon a naïve view of humans as altruistic and compassionate beings. Always alert to historical precedents, he ventures that, while love may have given rise to the creation of the great empires of classical antiquity, death drive ensured that they would all inevitably fall. The Soviet experiment and other communist utopian projects would fail, too, on account of a very fundamental Freudian principle: '[a]ggressiveness was not created by property. It reigned without limit in primitive times [...] it forms the basis of every relation of affection and love among people'.[19]

Despite his protestations, there are conceptual overlaps between Marx and the Freud of *Civilization and its Discontents*, arising out of Freud's own explication of cultural production. For Freud, psychological normality was indexed to an idea of social value through production: an aim of psychoanalysis was to revert the patient back to society. If we were to reframe the social theories of the late Freud in the language of Marx, Freud is interested in the way that civilization can sustain relations of capital and relations of production to maintain the longevity of the bourgeois mode of production. For Freud, the modern state safeguards the national modes of production by maintaining civilization through the implementation of a cultural superstructure, one element of which is cultural achievement. The survival of European civilization—Freud is writing not only against the backdrop of Soviet Russia but also the rise of National Socialism in Central Europe—depends upon an ability to ensure that the base modes of production can be maintained by a willing and capable population. If society is repressive and if, for its subjects, aim inhibition is hardwired into the structuration of reality, then Freud posits, like Marx, that this repression (or exploitation in Marxian terms) must be concealed. What Marx would call the cultural superstructure—art, philosophy, religion, literature and so on—Freudian theory, if not Freudian discourse, designates as part of culture. Culture becomes the site upon which an individual can re-cathect libidinal desire in the act of artistic creation, but it is also the location that conceals the ideology of the mode of production in order to secure its survival. This accounts for the manner in which Freud links aesthetics and art with ideas of law and order throughout *Civilization and its Discontents*. If civilization is responsible for an increasing discontent and the role of cultural production is to mediate between the masses and external reality, then Freud is here closer to Marx and Engels than he would care to admit. As Engels writes in a letter from 1890, 'the ultimately determining element in history is the production and reproduction of real life'.[20] It is their Hegelian influence that colors Marx and Engels's vision of society in a state of nature that, once liberated from the artifice of systems that cultivate false hierarchies and inequity, will finally be able to dedicate itself to forms of human fulfilment. Freud's stance is premised on what he perceives to be the nature of humans and their aggressive instincts. As death drive is ever present as a destructive force in the world and also tends towards a teleological end, humankind has erected an organizational system to mediate between their survival and their base natures. The cultural superego (or the state) functions as this mediating entity, which comprises both explicit prohibition in the form of cultural mores and legislative acts, and internalizing mechanisms that transmit cultural ideals. This organization of culture also serves to distract through sublimation, and to forge commonality through shared experience and a narcissistic enforcement that bands individuals together against the interests of their instinctual drives. Civilization mediates between humans and the hostility of the natural order, and the material production of that culture mediates individual interests within the collective repression of civilization.

In *An Autobiographical Study*, Freud discusses the shift throughout his later work from the individual to the social in terms that display a concern for the empirical: 'I should not like to create an impression that during this last period of my work I have turned my back upon patient observation and have abandoned myself entirely to speculation'.[21] Freud stresses that psychoanalysis has developed by way of empirical methods which can be repeated within a clinical setting, while simultaneously disavowing the proximity of his work to Western metaphysics: the culture of psychoanalysis is the scientific, the measurable and the repeatable, whereas philosophy lacks sufficient empirical rigor for it to be associated with psychoanalysis. As in his rejection of Marx and Engel's political philosophy, his insistence on the scientific, when taken alongside the denials of the philosophic, leads Freud to make an array of unconvincing claims in *An Autobiographical Study*. Among them is the profession that he 'carefully avoided any contact with philosophy proper' when he conceptualized psychoanalysis;[22] yet he admits that there are overlaps between his work and that of Schopenhauer and Nietzsche, two influences that he is then quick to elide:

> The large extent to which psycho-analysis coincides with the philosophy of Schopenhauer [...] is not to be traced to my acquaintance with his teaching. I read Schopenhauer very late in my life. Nietzsche, another philosopher whose guesses and intuitions often agree in the most astonishing way with the laborious findings of psycho-analysis, was for a long time avoided by me on that very account; I was less concerned with the question of priority than with keeping my mind unembarrassed.[23]

Freud's denial of philosophy inadvertently draws attention to another set of meanings attaching to the word 'culture', one that recalls a more biological etymology and metaphor: to cultivate, spawn or grow. Freud conceives of philosophy as an unscientific discourse that possesses the potential to intellectually contaminate and thus to delegitimize psychoanalysis's claims to scientific rigor, particularly as those claims were founded upon iterative labor. In his reading of Freud across his own work, Jacques Derrida uncovers psychoanalysis's debt to philosophy, such that in his reading analysis becomes philosophy at the margins. *The Post Card: From Socrates to Freud and Beyond* (1980) considers Freud's disavowal of philosophy as a gesture that, in the very act of avoidance, acknowledges its influence: '[w]hat is closest must be avoided, by virtue of its very proximity'.[24] Freud's denial marks his own anxiety that psychoanalysis be considered as a legitimate science founded on empirical methodologies, meaning that its influence on, and proximity to philosophy—and the reciprocal influence of philosophy upon it—must be denied in order to establish psychoanalysis as a radical episteme and disruption of scientific knowledge.

In his essay 'On Marx and Freud' (1991), Louis Althusser makes the claim that both figures framed in his title escaped the confines of their disciplines—political economy and psychology, respectively—and 'disturbed the universe [...] in which the bourgeois rose to power'.[25] Althusser's essay scans both Marxist and Freudian theory for useful ways to bring the two into closer theoretical contact in order to harness a relation that could be weaponized against bourgeois culture, and his Freud offers 'an example of a materialist and dialectical thought' via a rejection of the primacy of consciousness.[26] Psychoanalysis, according to Althusser, is a 'conflictual theory' not simply on account of its radicalism as a body of knowledge but according to how it has, since 'the times of its birth', incited resistances, annexations and revisions, which Althusser reads as the 'admission of its adversaries, [that psychoanalysis represents] something *true* and *dangerous*'.[27] The critical reaction that psychoanalysis incites is evidence of the way in which it undermines a classical philosophical position wherein individual consciousness is that which needs to be reconciled to cognitive, moral or transcendental systems of belief, while the philosophies of Kant, Locke and Hume represent modes of thinking that set out to reconcile individual consciousness with the external bourgeois reality that the subject inhabits or, in other words, present an ontological vision of subjects subordinated to an ideology that structures culture. Althusser argues that it is easier to recognize the ontological radicalism of Marx, as he 'dismantled the illusory unity of bourgeois ideology' by uncovering how individual consciousness is made to 'conform to its own ideological and political requirement'; or, in the language of classical Marxism, showed how an individual may be brought to class consciousness.[28] Althusser recognizes in Freud a similar epistemological intent to undermine the reconciliation of consciousness with ideology:

> Freud did not touch just *any* "sensitive point" in the existing philosophical, moral, and psychological ideology; the ideas that he upset were not there by chance, one fact of the development of human knowledge or illusion; thus, he did not touch merely a sensitive but secondary, localized point. Without knowing it at first (but he found out very quickly), he had touched *the most theoretically sensitive point* in the entire system of bourgeois ideology. The paradox is that Freud, apart from some schematic and questionable efforts (*Totem and Taboo*, *Civilization and its Discontents*, etc.) never really attempted to grasp and think as a whole this bourgeois ideology that he had struck in its most sensitive point.[29]

Freud's undermining of the consciousness-reality equation upon which Western civilization was structured accounts for the hostile reception of psychoanalysis by its critics, the conflictual nature of the practice considered dangerous in that it threatens the legitimacy of Western culture by exposing the consciousness-subject-ideology model as false. What for Althusser ultimately binds Marx's political economy together with Freudian psychoanalysis is the ability of both to undermine the entirety of that culture. Althusser draws attention to this revolutionary potential of Freudian theory by way of an apocryphal tale that recalls the moment when Freud, having arrived in the United States—the only trip he made outside of Europe—caught sight of the welcome party gathered at the harbor in New York and turned to his travel companion Jung:

> The words of Freud as he drew near to the United States are well known: "They don't realize that we are bringing them the plague." They remind us of Marx speaking of *Capital* as "a weapon aimed at the head of the bourgeoisie." These are the words of men who not only know what they are fighting but who also know that they bring to the world sciences that can only exist in and through struggle since the adversary cannot tolerate their existence: conflictual sciences without any possibility of compromise.[30]

This language of contagion makes explicit Freud's belief that psychoanalysis not only had the potential to radically alter the clinical or neuropsychological experience of patients, but also contained profound cultural implications. If we extend both logic and language, the United States was to be infiltrated and permanently transformed in the same way Europe had been in the aftermath of the inception and spread of Freudian psychoanalysis. Freud's repeated use of biological or cytological metaphors to explain his theories suggests an ambivalence in the way he imagines psychoanalysis as a biological agent that, like a plague, is loaded with the potential to colonize the dominant host culture. His characterization of psychoanalysis as a metaphorical plague equipped with the potential to reshape all aspects of US culture—its values, self-image, corporate and social behaviors—was prescient. In fact, as we have shown, the advent of globalization has meant that the social and psychological theories of the late Freudian corpus were instituted far beyond the practitioners' couches bordering Central Park, in the supranational bodies that give ideological shape to liberal capitalist democracy. Althusser thus exposes a latent paradox at the heart of the Freudian project: that the impulse towards destruction which lies beneath the civilized veneer of human nature and requires checking through increasingly interventionist forms of civilization is that which is potentially most radical in its implications for social revolution. If human nature was becoming increasingly difficult to control, then the only protection against an instinct towards destruction and chaos would be the advent of more civilization. In this instance then, the plague is not psychoanalysis, with its claims of unconscious libidinality, childhood sexuality and incestuous yearning, but a culture that mandates increasingly repressive forms of control.

'The Work of Culture'

Freud's late work may contain textual blanks relating to the influence of Western metaphysics on the codification of psychoanalytic theory, but these are rationalized via a commitment to maintaining the scientific integrity of the discipline: psychoanalytic culture was required to appear scientific in its language and methodologies precisely in order to legitimize its importance to the development of human understanding. The initial Freud wars, ironically, have their origins in a body founded by Freud and Sándor Ferenczi in 1910, The International Psychoanalytical Association (IPA). As it evolved out of the weekly meetings of the Wednesday Psychological Society hosted by Freud, the IPA transformed into the regulatory body for practitioners of Freud's theories and those who identified as Freudians; it also supervised the accreditation of officially endorsed psychoanalysts, to distinguish them from unscrupulous arrivistes and safeguard the discipline. And yet, arguably more than any detractors of Freudian theory, the IPA has throughout its history stoked and staged conflict within the psychoanalytic world. The Freud wars of the 1980s, and their reappearance in their current twenty-first century form, pale when measured against the internecine fallout that accompanied a defining stand-off in the history of psychoanalysis, one that would pit the Freud family and its loyal disciples against a radical heretic from Paris.

In the aftermath of Freud's death in the September of 1939 much acrimony was generated within psychoanalytic circles on account of the controversial role that the IPA began to assume in its overtly interventionist regulation of psychoanalytic practice. The origins of this dispute can be traced back to the IPA's post-Freudian leadership and its interpretation of a line delivered by Freud at the end of a lecture within a series later collected as the *New Introductory Lectures*, which it would subsequently adopt and systematically transform into a disciplinary *raison d'etre*.[31] In the lecture entitled 'The Dissection of the Psychical Personality', during which Freud first presented the sketch outlining his shift from a topographical towards a structural model of the unconscious—itself a development more radical than heretofore recognized—he also included the description of psychoanalysis as a therapeutic method that would later come to be interpreted as a mission statement. Freud states that:

> Its [psychoanalysis's] intention is [...] to strengthen the ego, to make it more independent of the super-ego, to widen its field of perception and enlarge its organization, so that it can appropriate fresh portions of the id. Where id was, there ego shall be. It is a work of culture—not unlike the draining of the Zuider Zee.[32]

This declaration, which Strachey translates from the original German *Wo Es war, soll Ich werden* ['[w]here id was, there ego shall be'], was interpreted as Freud's objective for psychoanalysis within the IPA.[33] In this declaration he appears simultaneously to inaugurate two principles: firstly, to situate the work of ego-strengthening as that of psychoanalysis and consequently to name it as taking place within culture; drawing on Freud's later theorizing, this would locate it within the realm of the reality principle, its achievements and strictures. Secondly, to align the task of ego-strengthening with the aim of psychoanalysis and hence to institute analysis as a cultural practice, meaning both within culture and pertaining to its theoretical dimensions, thus determining its future positioning and the legacy of Freud within psychoanalytic circles. Under the premiership of Anna Freud, the IPA consequently and aggressively promoted a vision of Freudianism that would equip the subject to better deal with quotidian life. According to its interpretation of Freud, analysts had a therapeutic responsibility to consciously bolster the ego of analysands in line with the edicts of the reality principle. The paradigm of Freudian analysis adopted by the IPA remained faithful to Freud's structural model and its dictate that the ego must satisfy the id while obeying the superego, but its belief in the establishment of the ego as the primary defense mechanism, and in this being the goal of psychoanalysis, was interpreted by many within the psychoanalytic community as an ideological stratagem. What we have identified as a consistent but implicit concern of early psychoanalysis with the individual as they functioned within society was replaced by a more explicit focus on the relation of the individual to the social via the IPA's commitment to 'ego-strengthening'. In this respect, the political shift that comes to define the work of the late Freud inadvertently also came to define psychoanalysis after his death.

As we have already established, though Freud may have opted for a public pose of political neutrality (albeit he retained a pride in Austrian imperialism), his theoretical discoveries would revolutionize the ideas and practice of politics in the early twentieth century. Despite claims of political as well as religious secularism in regard to everyday Viennese domestic affairs, our argument has highlighted how the social shift in Freud's writing coincided, especially in the latter years of his life, with an increased attention on geopolitical events. Moreover, and predating this turn, the founding of the IPA established Freud's political credentials in a more overt way. In light of Freud's forceful proclamations that psychoanalysis would not adopt any *Weltanschauung*, the decision to establish a regulatory body to administer psychoanalysis as it moved to become a global industry appears strangely contradictory. Why found an association with the remit to regulate the practicing of psychoanalysis unless the preservation of clinical integrity was a concern?. With its enlightened elite, loyal adherents and, after the founding of the IPA, the threat of punitive action, psychoanalysis resembled a religious order structured around a quasi-messianic leader figure. Freud's conviction in the discipline as a therapeutic instrument with the potential to generate a productive workforce, coupled with the writing on technique which was designed to preserve it against those who would corrupt it, testify to a twin desire that psychoanalysis not become tarnished by political sectarianism and that it be considered an international movement. Like the church missionary groups of the nineteenth century, the IPA emerged as the political wing of a doctrinal body of work that fostered similarly universalist ambitions. And just like an organized church, the IPA under the guidance of the holy father and his family harbored the ability to designate those who dissented from the official credo as apostates.

It is not by accident that we draw upon the language of organized religion when discussing the legacy of psychoanalysis after Freud's death. The organization was recognized within the international psychoanalytic community as the custodian of an orthodox Freudianism, but it was Jacques Lacan's critique of the IPA that would define psychoanalysis in the post-war era. Lacan's relationship with the IPA was always a fraught one, as he was skeptical of the followers who assumed the responsibility of controlling the theoretical purity of Freud's work after his death. In 1953, when he was head of the *Société Parisienne de Psychanalyse* (SPP), the French affiliate of the IPA, Lacan's anti-clericalism led to a vote of criticism in his leadership resulting from his use of 'the short session' in analysis, which contravened the fifty-minute length mandated by Freud himself. Lacan's fractious relationship with the psychoanalytic establishment continued to fester on for almost decade when, in 1964, the IPA annexed the leadership of the *Société Française de Psychanalyse* (SFP), a body that Lacan had formed having left the SPP, over the issue of bestowing accreditation upon analysts who had undergone training at the school in Paris; his ability to conduct analyses under its aegis was removed and he then established the *École Freudienne de Paris* (EFP) in 1964. The IPA set out to undermine Lacan and the ideas he was advancing due to its fear that his concentration on a radical strain within Freud's writing, concerned with emancipating individuals from repressive strictures and giving voice to the unconscious, was, in itself, non-Freudian. The IPA offered to recognize those trained as analysts by Lacan under the auspices of the SFP only on the proviso that he be removed from the institution that he had founded; at the heart of its complaint against Lacan was his refusal to submit to the IPA and Anna Freud's commitment to ego-strengthening as the *raison d'être* of any process of analysis. The IPA's insistence on strengthening the ego's defense mechanisms in line with the reality principle was in effect a means to redirect the desires of patients so as to allow them to assimilate fully into the emerging post-war ideology of capitalist democracy, whereas for Lacan the IPA's emphasis of 'where id was, there ego shall be' amounted to an ideological reading that diluted the emancipatory potential of Freud as a social theorist. He refuted the IPA's insistence that psychoanalysis could work towards a curative endpoint, believing that its interpretation and implementation of Freud's writing amounted to the imposition of a socially normative framework upon the individual that, for Lacan at least, represented the very antithesis of a discipline founded upon the pleasure principle. In a 1953 paper that was delivered in the Institute of Psychology at the University of Rome and which subsequently became known as the 'Rome Discourse', Lacan contests the claim that psychoanalysis has a teleological endpoint in ego-strengthening and the reassimilation of the subject to society, the outcome of which would function to return patients to the same world of systemic repression that generated their neuroses: '[a]nalysis can have as its goal only the advent of true speech and the subject's realization of his history in relation to a future'.[34] Lacan regarded Freud as a revolutionary because he was the first to provide a platform from which the unconscious could speak, but charged that psychoanalysis had become a form of repression implicated in the stifling of 'true speech', instead of being a therapy that gave expression to the unconscious. His call for a return to Freud was in fact a war cry demanding a return to the original text, prior to its interpretation and conversion into dogma—Lacan's commitment to this return entailed reading Freud in the original German—as well as to the contradictions and silences that Freud himself refused to remedy or fill.

In *Knowing, Not-Knowing, and Jouissance* (2018), his study into the feasibility of Freudian and Lacanian theory within a clinical environment, Raul Moncayo describes the institutional culture of the IPA during this time as resembling that of a church:

> Lacan disputed the doctrinal authority with which the psychoanalysts in the organization would concentrate all power within their own ranks, and exposed the psychoanalytic establishment as a ritualized, ceremonious and formulaic institution, not dissimilar to the self-perpetuating leadership of the Catholic priesthood or religious organizations.[35]

Moncayo takes his cue for this figurative reimagining of the IPA in terms of a church from Lacan himself, who wrote about his repeated expulsion from the IPA in a lecture entitled 'Excommunication', delivered to the *École Pratique des Hautes Études* with Claude Lévi-Strauss among the audience. In a typically colorful rhetorical construction, Lacan refers to his expulsion as his 'major excommunication' before alluding to the IPA as a religious organization under the doctrinal authority of Freud's daughter, Anna: 'I am not saying—though it would not be inconceivable—that the psycho-analytic community is a Church. Yet the question indubitably does arise—what is it in that community that is so reminiscent of religious practice?'.[36] Lacan consciously casts himself in the role of religious heretic, whose anti-clerical thinking has forced the adherents of a rigid orthodoxy to exile him from the main body of the institution. As part of his 'return to Freud' project, Lacan then revisits the central scene of *Totem and Taboo*, in which Freud proposes that guilt and shame arrive in the world via the parricide of the Primal Father, re-reading this scene in terms of how the sons internalize the approval/authority of the father figure, which leads Lacan to theorize the concept that he terms the 'name of the father' (*nom du père*). It is in this excommunication lecture, delivered on the occasion of having been banished from the SFP and, therefore, from psychoanalysis itself, that an overlap emerges between writing and biography, theory and praxis:

> How are we to understand the almost religious maintenance of the terms proposed by Freud to structure the analytic experience? Was Freud really the first and did he really remain the only theoretician of this supposed science to have fundamental concepts? Were this so, it would be very unusual in the history of the sciences.[37]

Lacan's heresy goes beyond undermining Anna as the daughter of Sigmund to question the sovereign authority of the Primal Father and symbolic Holy Ghost of psychoanalysis, Freud himself. His rebellion against the *nom du père* of the psychoanalytic community is consistent with his attack on psychoanalysis as it resists the uncovering of a 'true speech', through which the analysand would come to recognize their subjectivity in relation to the ideological and hegemonic apparatuses that structure their 'history in relation to a future'. This episode amounts to a desire on the part of the IPA to neurotically manage the development of psychoanalysis in an era in which its success and global reach made it increasingly difficult to do so; in it, Louis Althusser's observation of psychoanalysis as a 'conflictual' science finds further proof. Lacan's excommunication represents a historical period for psychoanalysis during which the IPA attempted to purge a troubling radicalism, the use of metaphors to describe it as a church or political party underscoring that it had come to be associated with and symbolically represent doctrinal orthodoxy. The irony is that in so becoming, the IPA had only succeeded in further establishing psychoanalysis as a science of controversy and one that was inherently controversial *qua* scientificity.

Mladen Dolar reads the event of Lacan's expulsion from the IPA as evidence of psychoanalysis's ability to generate disruption, suggesting that it continues to be of use as a method of reading culture precisely on account of its conflictual nature. Dolar is concerned with what becomes of psychoanalysis once radicals are expelled and conflict is eradicated, as 'conflict is its home ground; antagonism is the air it breathes'.[38] For Dolar, following Lacan, the forceful removal of dissenting voices however risks castrating psychoanalysis's power to disrupt. Seeking to venerate certain textual moments in Freud's work as the equivalent of psychoanalytic gospel truth, the IPA participated in the transformation of Freud from a figure of paradox, contradiction and conflict, to a neutered figure of historical curiosity. Dolar portrays the Freud culture industry (as we write we have a stuffed Freud doll perched at the end of a sofa) as representative of an impulse prevalent in the gentrification trend in late capitalism towards occupying and in the process sterilizing that which is deemed dangerous to the social order. He concludes that the IPA's desire to purge dissent was always destined to be counterproductive, as the synonymity of Freud with the discipline means that it will continue to elicit debate:

> The moment it is turned into a part of cultural heritage, the moment Freud is turned into a 'cultural hero,' or the moment it is part of the established clinical know-how, its edge is lost. One can draw some grim satisfaction from the fact that this move of gentrification has never quite succeeded, despite a century of efforts at domestication and pacification, so that the mere mention of Freud's name still tends to provoke controversy and disagreement.[39]

The veneration of Freud as the founding father of psychoanalysis seeks to detraumatize psychoanalysis by historicizing it as a stable and fixed epistemology, just as the IPA's commitment to Freud's work as the foundational scriptures upon which their church was to be built historicizes the figure of Freud, in such a way that it opens up the possibility for psychoanalysis to be appropriated by late capitalist ideology. In the world of today, Lacan's 'major excommunication' from the IPA represents a form of gentrification in its transformation of Freud into an establishment figure, but also a deeper intellectual gentrification as it turns heterodox epistemology into *doxa*, whether or not that move has been wholly successful. A century on from *Beyond the Pleasure Principle*, Freud's influence in the discipline of psychology as taught within the institution has waned. Undergraduate psychology courses recognize Freud's foundational importance to the field while simultaneously dismissing Freudian theory as primarily of historico-cultural significance; he has himself been excommunicated by modern psychology on account of a perceived clinical obsolescence, and the Freudian legacy has an institutional afterlife predominantly in Humanities departments. In his book *Freudian Repression: Conversation Creating the Unconscious* (1999), Michael Billig repeats something of an academic truism when he remarks that a 'student in literary studies' has a 'better chance of learning about Freud than does a student of psychology', though this exposure comes at a cost as, in the 'hands of literary experts, Freud has ceased to be a psychologist'.[40]

This book will be submitted by our respective institutions in the UK for the 2021 Research Excellence Framework (REF) and graded between one and four stars, largely on indicators designed to reward research considered to be of international or world-leading importance. The exercise, essentially a means by which the British Exchequer allocates state funding to universities in a sector that is rapidly moving away from a publicly funded model, defines the research interests of faculty members in UK Higher Education. Wendy Brown observes that one consequence of using a neoliberal model such as REF to gauge the importance of research in the Humanities is that it has led to the promulgation of work that becomes increasingly esoteric, in order to justify the awarding of a star rating in accordance with REF performance indicators of originality; she writes that such 'norms and practices render faculty research activity less relevant to teaching or to public knowledge and the public good than was the case even a generation ago'.[41] This is true of any academic discipline and not specific to the Humanities but, as a consequence of a collective institutional anxiety related to their relevance and competitive advantage in the market-driven economy, universities have capitulated and sought new ways to justify their existence in the eyes of the general public and to government funding bodies, instead of resisting and making a case for education as an inherent value to society. In the UK, research is additionally measured in terms of 'impact', a key performance indicator imposed upon the Humanities from STEM subjects. Defined in the REF guidelines as that which has 'an effect, change or benefit to the economy, society, culture, public policy or services, health, the environment or quality of life, beyond academia', the transformative impact of 'impact' as an important consideration in the research lives of faculty is one that is itself still to be fully measured.[42] While Brown is correct to conclude that the REF has had the paradoxical effect of producing work of an increasingly esoteric focus—and, in the Humanities, an increasingly material one, in line with the primacy of the empirical bias (book history, 'adjective + Humanities', material and print culture, oral histories, all aspects of the digital)—she does not explore at length the ways in which this has led to a new superego pressure towards justifying research in terms of the REF definition of impact. The weaponization of collaboration by metrics has led to the squaring of a circle wherein ever more niche research territories are circumscribed and presented in the vocabulary of the grant application along with their 'stakeholders', for the purpose of being able to apply for external funding to do the work that has been generated solely to apply for such funding and thus retain employment. This has resulted in a concentration of research that possesses a 'culture and heritage' dimension in line with the 'strategic priorities' of UK institutions, as it has been proven to be the most successful when it comes to making applications in what amounts to a professional form of a national lottery.

Mladen Dolar's warning that 'culture and heritage' inevitably coincides with an inability to threaten or disrupt authority is borne out by the research landscape within UK Humanities today, where it is no coincidence that heritage studies continues to make its ascent. Encompassing a wide array of periods and methodologies, heritage studies is a state-endorsed area of acceptable academic research which celebrates the uncovering and promotion of cultural signifiers that strengthen national mythologies, including those around the role in society of the Arts and Humanities, and ironically seeks to consolidate by cross-promoting the cultural sectors that this ideology itself places under threat. It is unsurprising that within this framework, the intellectual work of the Arts and Humanities is taken out of the university to supposedly ensure its survival and placed within that of the museum and heritage sectors. The continuum of a vaguely defined culture emblematizes the evacuation of education as value and direct social good and its replacement by education as measurable product, where its worth is estimated not as inherent but through its utility and proximity to other social institutions. The binary indicates a more profound tension around the purpose and aims of the modern university for which the predicament of the Arts, as it is subject to empirical bias and the imposition of market-driven logic, is a crucible.

The incompatibility of the REF definition of impact with Humanities research has compelled colleagues to form 'networks' with 'external partners' as a means to foster 'knowledge exchange', hopefully in the form of a tie-up with a local cultural institution and the development of an app to be targeted at the general public. Ultimately, then, the enshrining of 'impact' within the architecture of our lives as researchers represents a means of financially incentivizing, via grant capture, precisely the sort of research of which governments and university administrative structures approve, as well as tacitly endorsing the view of education from which this outcome is generated, one in which it requires a supplemental utility as its inherent utility is denied. In line with the valorization of evidence-based, data-driven work that mimics that of the sciences even where it may not produce research of intellectual value, the fetishistic impulse towards historicity has even extended to the intellectual card trick currently being played in English Literature departments throughout the world, wherein 'theory'—by which funding bodies really mean 'high theory'—has been transformed into a historical phenomenon deemed of little relevance to the world of today. This represents a recognition that theory remains a dangerous methodology and body of work for those in positions of social authority, both for its specific insights and for the symbolic principles of university education it endorses and upon which it is founded. It is significant that those of us who gravitate towards psychoanalytic theory to make sense of late capitalist culture might do so on the basis of an unconscious recognition that Althusser's characterization of it as a 'conflictual' science is correct, and that, for figures like Lacan, Dolar and others, the Humanities occupy a space outside the state-sponsored terrain of heritage that doubles as a shorthand for the mythological and the hegemonic. The demise of theory in the Humanities and the rise of a new New Historicism have resulted in another wave of intellectual gentrification that neuters the threat of disciplines and their outputs, which are ideally students endowed with the ability to recognize and reflect critically upon ideology. This charge is not new; Rousseau indicted the academy for its essentially civilizing function, observing that the central purpose of culture as disseminated through the sciences and arts is to lead out—educate—in order to bring in line:

> While government and laws provide for the safety and well-being of people in their collected life, the sciences, letters and arts—less despotic though perhaps more powerful—wrap garlands of flowers around the chains that weigh people down. They stifle the sense of freedom that people once had and for which they sensed that they were born, making them love their own servitude, and turning them into what is called a civilized people.[43]

The study of theory today might offer an outlet against the purpose of education as co-opted by the dominant social orders as its own work of culture, wherein the University function is to integrate subjects to civilization while providing the veil of cultural achievement that reconciles us to our assimilation.

Is There Any Escape?

The critique of mass culture under late capitalism by the Frankfurt School provided the basis for an understanding of the reification of art in popular cultural production and the co-opting of the aesthetic sphere, through technology, to a political function of sustaining the status quo of material conditions.[44] The postmodern episteme was subsequently defined by the symbiosis of late capital and culture, as postmodernism attained the status of a cultural dominant coterminous with and capable of reproducing the conditions of its production so that 'every position on postmodernism within culture', as Jameson writes, became 'also at one and the same time, and *necessarily*, an implicitly or explicitly political stance on the nature of multinational capitalism'.[45] How does cultural production and consumption in the neoliberal contemporary encode the relationship between work, leisure and the system, and what does it reveal to us about the political values inscribed in its forms?. The popularizing of the now obsolete Video Home System (VHS) in the 1980s transformed the consumption of visual culture in the Western world. Akin to the revolutions instigated by the advent of radio and the early sound technologies that appeared at the beginning of the twentieth century to be followed by television in its middle decades, VHS heralded a transformation in the commodification and dissemination of popular culture as living rooms across the world became personal cinemas, sites where the latest Hollywood blockbuster could be watched from the domestic comforts of the family sofa. This translocation to the domestic sphere of global cultural consumption realized the theoretical workings expressed by Freud in his essay 'The Uncanny' (1919), a staple text on English Literature programs across the world despite remaining largely ignored by those working in the clinical field. Home entertainment technologies—radio, TV, VHS and now today's streaming services—inadvertently instigated an *unheimlich* revolution within the home, exposing the ambivalence of domestic comfort by transmitting the cultural ideals filtered through popular form without the requisite shared experience. Psychoanalysis came out of the private and domestic spaces of late nineteenth-century Vienna: Freud's patients presented symptomologies that had their origins in the enclosed households of the European bourgeoisie, and they arrived at Freud's home to be cured. The actors who comprise the psychodrama of neurotic illness at an individual level are to be found in this space: the mother, the father and the central figure of the child. On the one hand, the new home entertainment technologies of the twentieth century disrupted the isolation of this domestic sphere by making it play host to global interests, and in doing so transformed the homely into the unhomely through technological invasion and the increasingly homogenized global political values that accompanied it. Yet when understood against this backdrop, VHS as a technology also encouraged the reclusive consumption wherein individuals eschewed communality to remain ensconced and, eventually, alienated, within the same repressive settings that psychoanalysis had established as a contributing source of neurotic pathology.

As video gave way to the increased data capacity of Digital Versatile Disc (DVD), this in turn initiated a cultural shift in the subject's relationship to the consumption of culture as it ushered in the era of the boxset and the phenomenon of binge-watching multi-volume tv series, precipitating a small-screen revolution whereby television attained the cultural status and corresponding budget previously reserved to cinema. Today, DVD has been rendered obsolete by streaming services such as Netflix, Amazon Prime and Apple TV+, which configure customers as the terminal nodal points plugged into archives of data that they are free to consume and 'curate' as a bespoke experience on demand. This continued move towards the ostensible democratization of culture stages certain psychoanalytic issues. Like the injunction to click through endless profile pictures and repetitively hit the like button on social media sites, multi-volume television participates in today's concentration capitalism as it rewards consumers with an appropriate pleasure by indulging a seemingly irrepressible need 'for just one more' episode; even so, what is now presented as unrestrained appetite is merely the rationed dispensing of a limited quota of enjoyment.

The ritualism that accompanies this mode of viewing and, indeed, the discourse of viewers, is also one that mimics the experience of an analysis: Freud's initial conception of the neurotic subject undergoing a process of daily sessions of analysis, five times a week for 50 minutes at a time, has been usurped by the ritualism of sitting down to watch (multiples of) the hour-long episode of the latest series. The fact that for twenty years we have languidly sprawled out across sofas in our homes to watch epic fantasies, New Jersey gangsters, corrupt Baltimore police detectives and Scandic noir, recalls the image of the Freudian patient lying upon the couch, and that so many of the most popular programs of recent history, and by virtue of that reasoning the most popular culture of our era—*The Sopranos*, *Mad Men* and so on—feature analysis in their narratives compounds the echoes of verisimilitude between the experience of binge watching and the analytic experience.[46] The manner in which popular visual media is consumed today reveals its psychic importance in the everyday lives of those living in the regions of the world where global capitalism allows its workers the illusion of free time, albeit that distinction is becoming increasingly blurred by the encouragement to permanent working mode enabled by supposedly flexible working practices. As the century progresses and cultural ideals increasingly reflect the ethos of free-market capitalism, this dispersal in terms of how we consume endorses and enforces the movement Adorno and Horkheimer first identified in their diagnosis of the Culture Industry towards late capitalist cultural values of a society of individuals. Correspondingly, the individualized experience of cultural consumption strengthens that subject position and the ideological values on which it rests. We can, on demand, tailor our consumer practice to watch a series in a matter of hours, while streaming a podcast, downloading a movie or album and uploading our own media to personal streaming platforms; this can also be happening simultaneously in other rooms of our homes, occupied by other individuals who are creating their own media ecologies. The hyper-consumerist impulse as it is translated to media enables popular culture to be proliferated through its technologies in the 'smart home', and increasingly on the body of the hybrid techno-subject, so that in our escapism we are further sequestered. Popular culture is increasingly and ironically anti-communal, popular in that it is widespread but not cohesive either experientially or temporally; in effect, what cohesion it now attains is more typically achieved through an alter/after life in other forms of media, for example in being taken out of context, shared and reiterated as memes.

The psychical, bodily and psychological demands that are omnipresent in the lives of late capitalist subjects have produced a curious response in consumers of contemporary culture. As we have outlined elsewhere in this book, the Freudian superego is the heir to the Oedipal stage of development, a repressive force that coerces the child to conform with the logic of bourgeois capitalist reality. Freud does not regard this in terms of an obvious negativity, in fact quite the contrary. For Freud, the repressive power of the superego plays a pivotal role in the formation of the infantile subject into an adult equipped with a morality and ethics in line with that of society. The superego's origins in, and subsequent association with, figures of authority who from the position of the child are understood as being representative of the dominant code of wider society, means that in the neoliberal moment superego guilt remains linked to social forms of performance anxiety. The Belgian psychoanalyst Paul Verhaeghe suggests in his 2012 book *What About Me?* that the superego dimension of today's globalized capitalism is becoming ever more aligned to an image of success mandated by advertising marketers. He depicts the symbols of achievement that structure the imagination of workers today as an illusion that serves a precise ideological purpose; success has become a 'yardstick' by which to gauge labor attributes that are vital to the maintenance of the global capitalist order: 'flexibility, speed, efficiency, results-orientedness, and articulateness in the sense of being able to sell yourself'.[47] Verhaeghe's work identifies how the late Freud's configuration of psychic normality to capitalist productivity—'[i]f success is the criterion of a normal identity, failure is the symptom of a disturbed one'—has been hardwired into the architectonic design of neoliberalism.[48] Verhaeghe participates in the theoretical schematizing of the Freudian superego that began with Freud, was opened up by Marcuse in respect of productivity and by Foucault in terms of an omnipresent form of surveillance, and has now been supercharged by a neo-Randian conception of success. Individual success must be broadcast to our neighbors, made materially visible in ways either nuanced (no logo) or crude (branded), extending to the type of culture that we consume in the privacy of the home made *unheimlich* by neoliberal values:

> If we look at what is expected at an individual level, the answer is "to enjoy life to the full". The person who best meets the norm is the one who enjoys the most, enjoyment being explicitly linked with consumption and products.[49]

Verhaeghe here recalls Lacan's retooling of the superego from a relentlessly punitive voice of prohibition to one mandating incessant enjoyment. Writing in mid-twentieth-century Paris, a very different cultural backdrop to Freud's long nineteenth-century version of Vienna, Lacan noticed a development in the injunctions of the superego that was reflective of a move towards greater social and sexual freedom. As Lacan observed in Seminar XX, '[n]othing forces anyone to enjoy except the superego. The superego is the imperative of jouissance—Enjoy!'[50] Writing in the legacy of Lacan, Todd McGowan avers that the 'rise of the superego and its demand for enjoyment is correlative to the transformation of a society of prohibition to a society of enjoyment'.[51] This developmental shift in the superego correlates to advancements in twentieth-century commodity capitalism, with over-production demanding new consumer markets. As we expand in our findings in our chapter on technology, the Freudian superego has undergone a further mutation in the era of digital capitalism. Instead of liberating us from a world of repressive prohibitions, Lacan's reworking of the superego in terms of an economy of enjoyment provides a blueprint to understand the cultural pathology of today.

There remains a sanctioned need for forms of psychic escape, whether in the everyday 'escapism' of leisure or in so-called guilty pleasures. In order to justify deviating from the established tastes an individual shares with the imagined community with which they associate, it has become customary to frame dissenting appetites in terms of a knowing irony; what are in fact mild irruptions of desire are reframed as guilty pleasure, but even these are increasingly appropriated to the mainstream as a form of branding through individualistic expression. Such normative transgressions through culture are now commonly justified in a language that simultaneously recognizes a sense of shame while also referencing the oppressive nature of contemporary life: I am only watching, reading, listening to, 'X' as a form of escapism. The phrasing acknowledges the fact that within late capitalist society there are no forms of psychic escape, only elusive possibilities. In Marx's original theory of labor, it was in the vested interest of a factory owner to provide his workers with an absolute minimum form of compensation for the labor provided, enough to feed themselves and any dependents who might eventually be incorporated into this hereditary system of exploitation, in order to ensure that the worker would return the next day. Marx's theory of surplus value is simply the profit that the owner of the means of production accrues after that point at which a worker has produced goods in excess of combined labor costs; if a nineteenth-century worker employed in the enterprise of making steam valves produces enough steam valves by eleven o'clock in the morning to feed themselves and their family for the day, then every valve produced until the close of the working day represents surplus value for the factory owner. This remains today; however, post-millennial culture offers a window into the shift from a consumer capitalism that now seems almost quaint to the finance capital that we now inhabit—that inhabits us—and cannot escape. There is no exit from the demands of a networked system and the culture it produces, especially where that culture appears to offer a respite from its commands. If we as workers today require scheduled moments of psychic liberation from the incessant dictates of capitalism to 'succeed' and 'enjoy', those interstices can only be experienced themselves as inherent to that system, updating Adorno and Horkheimer's observation that '[a]musement under late capitalism is the prolongation of work'.[52] Whereas for Adorno and Horkheimer mass culture was integral to working life because it was 'sought after as an escape from the mechanized work process, and to recruit strength in order to be able to cope with it again', the contemporary consumer-subject lives within incessant flows of information.[53] Our utilizing of devices engenders a mode of constant reception that collapses the distinction between categories of data and between work and leisure. The co-existence of work and leisure, facilitated by the contemporary dispersal of work beyond fixed time and place, recognizes the totalizing aspect of digital capitalism as it is designed to network the subject into capital at all times and eventually to facilitate the production of the subject as networked human capital.

What lies beyond the pleasure principle, as Freud schematizes it, is the existence of a drive that, on first reading, appears to work *contra* to the pleasure principle. His theorizing of the death drive is the moment that Freud places psychoanalysis into a state of crisis, the potential threat that it poses to the entirety of his life's work the ultimate validation of Althusser's assessment of psychoanalysis as a 'conflictual theory'. Freud characterizes this 'daemonic force' as 'a universal attribute' that predates the beginning of all organic life ('*inanimate things existed before living ones*').[54] An often-disregarded element of death drive is its tendency towards an organization of sorts: '[the] aim of all life is death'.[55] Once again parallels can be detected between the work of Marx and Freud as triangulated through Hegel (indeed, Freud discusses Hegelian notions of time in the text), for the death drive is presented as possessing a teleological dimension. Just as capitalism is working towards its own demise, so too, Freud argues, is all of life under the sway of this drive to destruction. Psychoanalysis in this new era of death drive is imagined by Freud, quoting the poet Friedrich Rückert, as bearing a resemblance to the war-wounded patient: [*w*]*as man nicht erfliegen kann, muss man erhinken/* [...] *Die Schrift sagt, es ist keine Sünde zu hinken*, translated by Strachey as '[w]hat we cannot reach flying we must reach limping/ [...] The Book tells us it is no sin to limp'.[56]

Once again, as he does in *Totem and Taboo*, *The Future of an Illusion* and *Civilization and Its Discontents*, Freud reveals the tension between human nature and the cultural output that emerges to mediate between us and civilization, as one in which their mastery over nature has allowed humans to devise further mechanisms to thwart death drive from ever gaining full expression. Although discussed more fully in *Civilization and Its Discontents*, *Beyond the Pleasure Principle* traces the anatomy of the pleasure principle to its logical endpoint: what would happen if it were to be given absolute expression?. This question initiates Freud's theorizing of a drive beyond the pleasure principle: if humans were to be returned to the state of nature, wherein there would be no checks on our ability to give expression to this incessant desire for pleasure, Freud predicts that this would inevitably result in a form of pleasure that necessitates death. In *Beyond the Pleasure Principle*, Freud gestures to a paradox within the pleasure principle to which he had hitherto been oblivious, namely that full articulation of the pleasure principle leads to the end of life:

> The pleasure principle seems actually to serve the death instincts. It is true that it keeps watch upon stimuli from without, which are regarded as dangers by both kinds of instincts; but it is more especially on guard against increases of stimulation from within, which could make the task of living more difficult.[57]

The economics of the pleasure principle are simple enough: the attainment of pleasure yielded is directly proportional to the amount of energy that is psychically expended by the individual, therefore a complete realization of pleasure would necessitate the release of an energy so strong that it would result in death. The pleasure principle, that founding ideal of the psychoanalytic project, is revealed in this later work as a drive that yearns for the optimal release of pleasure at all times, and the reality principle rendered secondary to this need for pleasure. This paradox—that absolute pleasure would necessitate absolute destruction—means that repetition is not a feature of the pleasure principle. What lies beyond the pleasure principle is the drive to return to inanimate life. Freud employs biological models that exhibit the influence of Darwinian evolutionary science to explain how life can be possible at all, if the aim of all life is death. It is death drive that explains the seemingly random nature of natural selection and the establishment of culture that allows for the germination of life:

> For a long time, perhaps, living substance was thus being constantly created afresh and easily dying, till decisive external influences altered in such a way as to oblige the still surviving substance to diverge ever more widely from its original course of life and make ever more complicated *détours* before reaching its aim of death. These circuitous paths to death, faithfully kept to by the conservative instincts, would thus present us to-day with the picture of the phenomena of life.[58]

Civilization is the means by which death drive is structured via a networked system that sustains life through the deferral of destruction—what Freud refers to as *détours*. The enjoyment of culture represents the ultimate embodiment of the Freudian *détour*, creating a space whereby a subject cathects a quota of death drive in a manner deemed permissible. To repeat a formulation that we offered earlier in this chapter, for the late Freud it is cultural superego (or the state) that assumes a primary role in mediating between subjects and their base natures. In order for humans to tolerate this mediation, culture—as expressed in what Freud terms the artistic achievements of civilization, such as art, film or music—is necessary as a means to distract from this inhibiting of the aim and serves a further inhibiting function.

Of all the late Freud's visions of civilization the one that is presented in *Beyond the Pleasure Principle* is the most radical, that of a society imagined as a vast circuit board and culture as the resistors. We have already shown in chapter two the significance of Freud's belief that civilization is only possible after a renunciation of instinct, and considered how this can be redirected when individual autonomy is surrendered through aligning with a mass of people; however, the blueprint of civilization as a system of distractions and prohibitions that emerges in *Beyond the Pleasure Principle* stresses the perpetual precarity upon which the entire social system is predicated. This circuitous design of a vast living architecture—Freud's vision here anticipates the cybernetic systems of the mid twentieth century—is responsible for the repetitive nature of behaviors or a symptomology that arises from a stifling of death drive. Repetition as an expression of death drive begins to attain crucial significance when understood against such late discoveries within Freud's metapsychology. Repetition emerges as both a symptom of death drive and, paradoxically, the primary psychic means to defer it; or, to phrase it slightly differently, repetition can be utilized as a means of ego-strengthening that remains steadfast to the Freudian maxim that became the dictate of the IPA under Anna's reign. Ultimately, this is the lesson Freud derives from the play of his Grandson Ernst: that the *unheimlich* can be rendered *heimlich* when the subject achieves a degree of mastering the *détournement* of *todestrieb*. *Fort/da* amounts to Ernst learning how to redirect death drive via a system of repetitive deferral; Freud writes that 'children repeat unpleasurable experiences' so that they 'can master a powerful impression far more thoroughly by being active than they could by merely experiencing it passively. Each fresh repetition seems to strengthen the mastery they are in search of'.[59] Repetition becomes a way to orientate and negotiate daily life, and this configuration of repetition as a mastery over anxiety imbues with significance those nightly, domestic rituals we now undertake to make life bearable in the twenty-first century: the cyclical organization of our free time in which we consume cultural outputs outside of the workplace amounts to the contemporary equivalent of Little Ernst's *fort/da* play with the bobbin. In order to reappear [*da*] at work in the morning, we require to make ourselves gone [*fort*] by retreating into a world of cultural consumption. A psychoanalytic understanding of the so-called work-life balance reveals the logic that underpins it to be nothing more than a superstructural investment in free time and cultural consumption that masks the stratagems of Human Resource philosophy devised to extract maximum productivity from the global workforce.

The competing image of repetition that emerges in *Beyond the Pleasure Principle* is that in which the quota of unpleasure generated overwhelms the subject so that they become a living emblem of the destructive energy of death drive. Instead of being a signal for a repetition that enables a mastery of unconscious anxiety, this form of repetitive behavior is far more neurotic and, Freud believed, had its origins in repressed infantile memory: '[i]t is clear that the greater part of what is re-experienced under the compulsion to repeat must cause the ego unpleasure, since it brings to light activities of repressed instinctual impulses'.[60] The portrait of the late Freud that emerges in *Beyond the Pleasure Principle*, for all his insistence on speculation and a reluctance to fully trace the repercussion of his most disruptive discovery, is of one who appears convinced of the truth value of death drive. Freud establishes death drive as a fundamental principle akin to Einstein's theory of relativity, and a phenomenon discernible in everyday life. He examines how, wherever repetition is detected, we are in the presence of death drive: in our individual relationships, professional lives and in the culture which he nominates the primary means to encourage a form of social conjugation with the civilization we have erected in order to prevent a full realization of the death drive. Repetition is extant within the most intimate of our interpersonal relations, Freud observing that 'based upon behavior in the transference and upon life-histories of men and women, we shall find courage to assume that there really does exist in the mind a compulsion to repeat, which overrides the pleasure principle'.[61] The social turn in the Freud's late work is more than a scholarly *détour* that he makes away from the individual to culture, but is rather indicative of how he pioneered a vision of society as a networked system featuring actors whose interconnectivity is determined by invisible, unconscious, forces. Having made this turn, he is then able to observe the frequency and prevalence of repetition as fundamental to the structuring of life. Freud's schematizing of death drive as a teleological force, the incessant impulse towards destruction as the psychic engine that propels progress, is immediately counteracted by the way in which civilization and its material and sensory culture have been designed to ward off its destructive energy.

Beginning with the stance of postmodern irony and repetition, we see evidence of Freud's claims into and beyond the first decades of the twenty-first century. Although in our present manifestation of late capitalism there is a sense of aesthetics seeking to return to the consolation of humanist values, as exemplified for instance in the post-postmodernism of the 'new sincerity' and metamodernist movement, this is coupled with a legacy of ironic detachment and also with the continued erasure of macro-social critique as cultural production focuses on the individual as the site of resistance. With regard to popular culture, Hollywood and middle-brow popular fiction increasingly appears as a form of repetition compulsion: while it has throughout its history consistently recycled material and tropes, contemporary cinema is epitomized by the celebration of the remake or, in the language of marketing, the franchising of universes. In terms of Freud's repetition compulsion, does this endless remaking and reiteration of characters not evidence the presence of death drive within today's society?. One simple reading, following on from Freud's work on creative writing, is that the spectacle of Hollywood film has always provided a space for a form of vicarious identification to be facilitated. The film-going or tv-watching subject is then able to covertly discharge a quotient of libidinal desire, be that sexual or aggressive. This is the fantasy dimension of Hollywood as imagined in terms of its early origins as a dream factory of sorts. When read against the exhaustion that we can discern in the ritualistic and repetitive way that television is now consumed, and in the language of escapism that is presented as a cultural alibi, the spectacular element of modern CGI cinema serves a valuable psychic function in the contemporary world, further inuring us to our position. Repetition, functioning much like the canned laughter of previous decades, is dependent upon the perpetuation of *heimlich* cultural themes, tropes and figures; it evidences the presence of a drive towards destruction, a move towards cultural annihilation that is prolonged via detours forged by the pleasure principle.

Forms of high culture are also now implicated in this logic. Where avant-garde art exists and where it makes the economic system and its ideological dissemination visible by offering a critique of the system, including an implicit critique of its own status within that system as commodity, it has also been assimilated to neoliberal market logic as an object of culture. The strength of the modern art economy, and its status as a traded commodity within the global economy, leads into absurdist territory wherein artworks that make of their commodification their subject attain the value on the market of a pure ideal, formalized. While works of modern art may offer the same sort of substitutive pleasure of renunciation identified by Freud, the question is whether their viewing prohibits rather than stirs us to action, because it offers an experience of solidarity that allows us to recognize our own dissatisfaction in that of others and thus to release it. It offers a complication to Freud's theory of the compensation of culture, making us aware of our discontent under the ideals by which we are forced to live, but offering us compensation for the renunciation of our drives, which might otherwise result in its overthrow, by means of a dual interplay. In this, we are given an aesthetic experience that offers pleasure by virtue of its appeal (including by accrual of cultural capital) and allowed concurrently to be brought into contact with the source of our dissatisfaction and to discharge a quota of aggression towards it through the sublimation of the work of art. Rather than militating, cultural production mediates renunciation to that culture it represents. When the role of the object is no longer to celebrate cultural ideals, yet when even its ability to critique is compromised by a limited capacity only to reflect or present, then we might ask whether even apparently radical culture further demonstrates the impossibility of exit from the current system.

Notes

1. Freud (1964b, p. 144).
2. Freud (1964d, p. 6).
3. James Strachey, 'Editor's Note', from Sigmund Freud, *The Future of an Illusion*, in *The Standard Edition of the Complete Psychological Works of Sigmund Freud,* trans. by James Strachey, Vol. XXI (London: Hogarth Press, 1964d [1927]), pp. 3–4 (4).
4. Freud (1964b, p. 89).
5. Freud (1964b, p. 79).
6. Freud (1964b, p. 80).
7. Freud (1964b, pp. 80–1).
8. Freud (1964b, p. 81).
9. Ibid.
10. Freud (1964b, p. 13).
11. Freud (1964b, pp. 13–4).
12. Freud (1964b, p. 14).
13. Freud (1964b, p. 92).
14. Freud (1964b, p. 93).
15. Freud (1964b, p. 94).

16. Freud (1964b, p. 112).
17. Freud (1964b, p. 112).
18. Freud (1964b, p. 113).
19. Ibid.
20. Friedrich Engels to J. Bloch, 1890: https://www.marxists.org/archive/marx/works/1890/letters/90_09_21.htm
21. Sigmund Freud (1959a, p. 59). We do not have space to concentrate on Freud's use of the 'speculation' here, but, as Derrida observes in his writing on Freud in *The Post Card*, it becomes intrinsic to the late Freud's method. Speculation, as used by Freud, is a means by which he can safeguard himself from potential criticism in the face of some of his more contentious theories. Freud speculates in such a way that he also ensures his own importance to the discipline of psychoanalysis as he grows older. His speculations are perpetual provocations that require his presence to resolve. Jacques Derrida, *The Post Card: From Socrates to Freud and Beyond*, trans. by Alan Bass (Chicago, IL: University of Chicago Press, 1987 [1980]).
22. Freud (1959a, p. 59).
23. Freud (1959a, pp. 59–60). Indeed, Peter Gay directly contradicts Freud's claims in *Beyond* when detailing how he was under the sway of Schopenhauer while formulating his theory of drive: '[o]ne remembers what Freud had told his friend Lou Andreas-Salomé in the summer of 1919: he had stumbled onto a strange idea via the drives and was reading all sorts of things, including Schopenhauer. The result was his vision of two elemental pugnacious forces in the mind, Eros and Thanatos, locked in eternal battle'. Gay (1995, p. 401).
24. Derrida (1987, p. 263).
25. Louis Althusser, 'On Marx and Freud', trans. by Warren Montag, *Rethinking Marxism*, 4:1, (1991), pp. 17–30 (17).
26. Althusser (1991, p. 19).
27. Ibid.
28. Althusser (1991, p. 25).
29. Althusser (1991, p. 25).
30. Althusser (1991, p. 26).
31. Freud (1964c, p. 80).
32. See Freud (1964c, p. 80).
33. The translation has been open to debate, most notably where Lacan takes exception to the privileging of ego authority over the id. See Lacan, 'The Freudian Thing, or the Meaning of the Return to Freud in Psychoanalysis', in *Écrits*, trans. by Bruce Fink (New York, NY: W.W. Norton & Company, 2006 [1966]), pp. 334–63.

34. Jacques Lacan, 'The Function and Field of Speech and Language in Psychoanalysis', in *Écrits*, trans. by Bruce Fink (New York, NY: W.W. Norton & Company, 2006 [1966]), pp. 197–268 (249).
35. Raul Moncayo, *Knowing, Not-Knowing, and Jouissance: Levels, Symbols, and Codes of Experience in Psychoanalysis* (New York, NY: Palgrave Macmillan, 2018), p. 236.
36. Jacques Lacan, *The Four Fundamental Concepts of Psycho-Analysis*, ed. by Jacques-Alain Miller and trans. by Alan Sheridan (London: The Hogarth Press, 1977 [1973]), p. 3; p. 4.
37. Lacan (1977, p. 10).
38. Dolar (2008, p. 19).
39. Ibid.
40. Michael Billig, *Freudian Repression: Conversation Creating the Unconscious* (Cambridge: Cambridge University Press, 1999), p. 2.
41. Brown (2015, p. 196).
42. Research Excellence Framework 2011.
43. Jean-Jacques Rousseau, *The First Discourse: Discourse on the Sciences and Arts*, ed. and trans. by Susan Dunn (New Haven, CT: Yale University Press, 2002 [1750]), pp. 43–68 (49).
44. Theodor W. Adorno and Max Horkheimer, 'The Culture Industry: Enlightenment as Mass Deception', in *Dialectic of Enlightenment*, trans. by John Cumming (London and New York, NY: Verso, 1997 [1947]), pp. 120–67.
45. Jameson (1991, pp. 3–4).
46. Even the clichéd figure of the doctor as medical hierophant as it is routinely performed on shows like *In Treatment* (itself based on an Israeli progenitor, *BeTipul*), *House*, *The Good Doctor* and *Hannibal* owes a cultural legacy to the Freudian doctor. NBC's drama *Hannibal* stages the analyst/therapist and analysand/patient relationship as one of cannibal serial-killer peril. The exaggerated European sophistication of Hannibal, played by Mads Mikkelsen, consciously recalls the original reception of psychoanalysis as an arcane European science. The early episodes of the show hinge upon Hannibal's ability to manipulate the transference period, or the equivalent of it, in order to exert a sovereign control over Will Graham, played by Hugh Dancy. In depicting the analyst/analysand relationship as one in which the latter is shown to be vulnerable to the psychic superiority of the former, *Hannibal* recalls early anxieties of psychoanalysis as a somatic discipline that originated out of the Central European tradition of mesmerism.
47. Paul Verhaeghe, *What About Me? The Struggle for Identity in a Market-Based Society*, trans. by Jane Hedley-Prôle (London: Scribe Publications, 2014 [2012]), p. 201.
48. Ibid.

49. Verhaeghe (2012, pp. 200, 201).
50. Jacques Lacan, *The Seminar, Book XX, Encore 1972-1973: On Feminine Sexuality, the Limits of Love and Knowledge*, ed. by Jacques-Alain Miller and trans. by Bruce Fink (New York, NY: W.W. Norton & Company, 1998 [1975]), p. 3.
51. Todd McGowan, *The End of Dissatisfaction?: Jacques Lacan and the Emerging Enjoyment Society* (Albany, NY: State University of New York, 2004), p. 30.
52. Adorno and Horkheimer (1997, p. 137).
53. Ibid.
54. Sigmund Freud, *Beyond the Pleasure Principle*, in *The Standard Edition of the Complete Psychological Works of Sigmund Freud*, trans. by James Strachey, Vol. XVIII (London: Hogarth Press, 1955c [1920]), pp.1–64 (35; 36).
55. Freud (1955c, p. 36).
56. Freud (1955c, p. 64).
57. Freud (1955c, p. 63).
58. Freud (1955c, pp. 38–9).
59. Freud (1955c, p. 35).
60. Freud (1955c, p. 20).
61. Freud (1955c, p. 22).

Works Cited

Theodor W. Adorno and Max Horkheimer, 'The Culture Industry: Enlightenment as Mass Deception', in *Dialectic of Enlightenment*, trans. by John Cumming (London and New York, NY: Verso, 1997 [1947]).

Louis Althusser, 'On Marx and Freud', trans. by Warren Montag, *Rethinking Marxism*, 4:1, (1991).

Michael Billig, *Freudian Repression: Conversation Creating the Unconscious* (Cambridge: Cambridge University Press, 1999).

Wendy Brown, *Undoing the Demos: Neoliberalism's Stealth Revolution* (New York, NY: Zone Books, 2015).

Jacques Derrida, *The Post Card: From Socrates to Freud and Beyond*, trans. by Alan Bass (Chicago, IL: University of Chicago Press, 1987 [1980]).

Mladen Dolar, 'Freud and the Political', *Harvard Journal of the Legal Left*, Vol. 4:15 (2008).

Sigmund Freud, *Beyond the Pleasure Principle*, in *The Standard Edition of the Complete Psychological Works of Sigmund Freud*, trans. by James Strachey, Vol. XVIII (London: Hogarth Press, 1955 [1920]).

Sigmund Freud, *An Autobiographical Study*, in *The Standard Edition of the Complete Psychological Works of Sigmund Freud*, trans. by James Strachey, Vol. XX (London: Hogarth Press, 1959 [1925]).
Sigmund Freud, *Civilization and Its Discontents*, in *The Standard Edition of the Complete Psychological Works of Sigmund Freud*, trans. by James Strachey, Vol. XXI (London: Hogarth Press, 1964 [1930]).
Sigmund Freud, *The Future of an Illusion*, in *The Standard Edition of the Complete Psychological Works of Sigmund Freud*, trans. by James Strachey, Vol. XXI (London: Hogarth Press, 1964 [1927]).
Sigmund Freud, *New Introductory Lectures on Psychoanalysis*, in *The Standard Edition of the Complete Psychological Works of Sigmund Freud*, trans. by James Strachey, Vol. XXII (London: Hogarth Press, 1964 [1933]).
Peter Gay, *Freud: A Life for our Time* (London: Papermac, 1995 [1988]).
David Harvey, *A Brief History of Neoliberalism* (Oxford and New York, NY: Oxford University Press, 2005).
Fredric Jameson, *Postmodernism: Or, the Cultural Logic of Late Capitalism* (Durham, NC: Duke University Press, 1991).
Jacques Lacan, *The Four Fundamental Concepts of Psycho-Analysis*, ed. by Jacques-Alain Miller, trans. by Alan Sheridan (London: The Hogarth Press, 1977 [1973]).
Jacques Lacan, *The Seminar, Book XX, Encore 1972–1973: On Feminine Sexuality, the Limits of Love and Knowledge*, ed. by Jacques-Alain Miller and trans. by Bruce Fink (New York, NY: W.W. Norton & Company, 1998 [1975]).
Jacques Lacan, 'The Function and Field of Speech and Language in Psychoanalysis', in *Écrits*, trans. by Bruce Fink (New York, NY: W.W. Norton & Company, 2006 [1966]).
Jacques Lacan, 'The Freudian Thing, or the Meaning of the Return to Freud in Psychoanalysis', in *Écrits*, trans. by Bruce Fink (New York, NY: W.W. Norton & Company, 2006 [1966]).
Todd McGowan, *The End of Dissatisfaction?: Jacques Lacan and the Emerging Enjoyment Society* (Albany, NY: State University of New York, 2004).
Raul Moncayo, *Knowing, Not-Knowing, and Jouissance: Levels, Symbols, and Codes of Experience in Psychoanalysis* (New York, NY: Palgrave Macmillan, 2018).
Jean-Jacques Rousseau, *The First Discourse: Discourse on the Sciences and Arts*, ed. and trans. by Susan Dunn (New Haven, CT: Yale University Press, 2002 [1750]).
Paul Verhaeghe, *What About Me? The Struggle for Identity in a Market-Based Society*, trans. by Jane Hedley-Prôle (London: Scribe Publications, 2014 [2012]).

CHAPTER 6

Conclusion: Death Drive Ecologies

During the 2008 financial crisis, it became normal to hear economic commentators discuss the markets as if they were sentient. We were constantly being updated on the nightly news with regard to how financial markets were reacting with worry, or nervousness, or anxiety, as a crisis that had its origins in subprime mortgages unfolded on our phones, tablets and televisions. When political leaders were galvanized to begin an intergovernmental process of nationalizing private debt across Europe and America via the central banking system, a policy that was camouflaged in the technocratic language of quantitative easing and stimulus packages, economic editors would inform viewers that markets were reacting optimistically or with a sense of hope. The importation of a language that accords sentience to financial systems echoes Lacan's emphasis on the automated character of death drive. From a Lacanian position, do such linguistic strategies of anthropomorphization not reveal an undead aspect to the financial markets today?. High-frequency trading, the practice of buying equities or commodities by machines and then reselling it at a higher cost within a few milliseconds, requires reaction speeds beyond human capability. Today the vast majority of financial transactions that comprise that entity we collectively conceptualize as the market are conducted by machines powered by algorithms that are beyond the cognitive comprehension of human users. The term 'uncanny valley' was first coined by robotics engineers to describe the affective point at which cyborgs began to generate unease within human subjects on account of their human similitude, from which

M.-D. Dick, R. McLaughlan, *Late Capitalist Freud in Literary, Cultural, and Political Theory*,
https://doi.org/10.1007/978-3-030-47194-1_6

they posited that humans refuse empathetic identification with a machine precisely at the moment it becomes indistinguishable from human life. To counteract this, engineers purposely bestow a degree of artificiality on to their constructs in order to instate a perceptible difference and distance in AI from human life. The anthropomorphizing of the world financial markets reverses this idea, in that human anxiety relates to the system's apparent independent animation so that the impulse to anthropomorphize becomes a means to psychologically safeguard the limits of our understanding through the projection of human qualities upon inanimate operations. To accord sentience to the insensible algorithmic logic of markets evidences a psychic and discursive desire to control the unease that their inhumanity, and all that it entails, generates. It performs an illusion of control over a system that has gone beyond human regulation and comprehension, other than turning the machines on or off. Imagining financial markets as cognizant would explain the seemingly capricious and inconsistent patterns generated by the world of digital finance and collectively disavows the inhuman and inhumane aspects of global capitalism. It becomes psychologically more tolerable to outsource responsibility for a system that continues to generate inequity, poverty and death, if capitalism itself is reimagined as possessing a singular consciousness.

Making a return of our own to a quotation already introduced in chapter three, Deleuze and Guattari fall into this anthropomorphizing trap when they mobilize the language of mental illness to explain the operational logic of capitalism through its financial system:

> Underneath all reason lies delirium drift. Everything is rational in capitalism, except capital or capitalism itself. The stock market is certainly rational; one can understand it, study it, the capitalists know how to use it, and yet it is completely delirious, it's mad.[1]

After Freud, however, the repetitive oscillating patterns that continue to define capitalism as a financial system testify to the presence of death drive within its economic models. For Lacanians such as Žižek, capitalism is a zombie or undead system that survives through its ability to defer the destructive tendencies of libido articulation. Yet what such an interpretation of Freudian death drive neglects to properly account for is its teleological dimension. Freud conceptualizes the entirety of human history as evidence of the reality of death drive and consequently views all human progress as propelled by it; as he develops the theory of death drive, he comes to see it as advancing ultimately towards annihilation. Death drive displaces Marx's historical materialism and class conflict as the primary motivator of progress. Whereas formerly the pleasure principle seemed to be associated with creation, Freud's late work directly associates creation with death drive and relegates the pleasure principle to the erotic dimension of the drive towards destruction. It is death drive that builds civilizations, and it is death drive that destroys empires. Freud theorizes death drive as the organizing principle of all life; within our current understanding of the migration from human to machine agency, it is increasingly difficult to culturally and collectively deny its existence as that which animates the entire system. It becomes futile to distinguish between various forms or sub-iterations of free-market capitalism—predatory, conscientious, green and so on—as, when understood within a psychoanalytic paradigm, all capitalism is disaster capitalism tending towards destruction.

In the section from the *Grundrisse* that is known as 'The Fragment on Machines' (1858), Marx reveals the ontological repercussions of mechanized labor as it transforms humans into 'conscious linkages' during the process of commodity production.[2] Both Marx and Freud's theories share a teleological aspect. The former dictates that advancements in the instruments of production would revolutionize all social relations and institute a change in the dominant mode of production. Marx hypothesizes that the mode of production would be one in which relations of production or labor would be increasingly defined by industrial capitalism's generation of surplus value through automation. Yet even when pessimistically assessing the ontological and economic reality of the majority toiling under the productive pressures of the capitalist mode of production, Marx's Hegelianism means that he is able to discern an optimism within the industrial sublime created through automation. While humans may be relegated to nodal points within a network of commodity production and capital exchange, the interconnectivity of this network, the increasingly centralized nature of the means of production and the generation of an increasingly redundant, but discontent, proletariat, allowed Marx to conclude that '[c]apital thus works towards its own dissolution as the form dominating production'.[3]

Marx's economic philosophy fails to accommodate the presence of death drive within organic and inorganic life. He believed that if the external world could be bent towards human benefit and the establishment of mechanical systems tame the hostility of nature, then humans would interact rationally and human nature be allowed to flourish. Marx understood sister's deathbed while possessed by a desire for her brother-in law: '[n]ow he [her brother-in-law] is free and can marry me'.[10] The neurotic reaction, according to Freud, would be to instantly repress the desire for her dying sister's husband, only for it to return as symptom in the 'hysterical pains' that she presented to him later as a patient; the psychotic reaction, however, would have involved sacrificing a fragment of reality via the production of a delusion that would have disavowed her desire.[11] By way of this historical return to Elisabeth von R, the late Freud finds a case history that schematizes the distinction between neurosis and psychosis via a third topographical marker identified as 'reality': 'neurosis does not disavow the reality, it only ignores it; psychosis disavows it and tries to replace it'.[12] The distinction is that unlike neurosis, which does not involve the outright denial of reality, psychosis not only disavows reality but replaces it with fantasy to become the mode by which the subject interacts with and mediates the external world.

In his 1937 'Constructions in Analysis' Freud completes his work on neurosis and psychosis by investigating the nature of the fantasies that come to stand between the psychotic subject and lived reality and, true to the late Freud's tendency towards disruption, collapses the distinction between the two mental states. The Freud of 'Constructions in Analysis' identifies how the fantasy that replaces the forfeiture of reality by the psychotic is a 'fragment of *historical truth*' that originates from an unconscious reservoir of 'infantile sources'.[13] Contrary to an early psychoanalytic belief—and the one held by Deleuze and Guattari—that posited psychotics as unsuitable for analysis, Freud reveals how psychotic fantasies have their origins in the repressed 'reminiscences' from childhood, which, presumably, leaves open the rehabilitative promise of psychoanalysis.[14] Yet what is important for the late Freud is the configuration of the psychotic individual as relinquishing a fragment of reality in favor of the id and replacing this psychic deficit via the construction of fantasy. The concluding paragraph of 'Constructions in Analysis' features a now familiar turn towards the social and his belief that civilization displays behavioral attributes or tendencies that bear comparison to the psychotic patient: '[i]f we consider mankind as a whole and substitute it for the single human individual, we discover that it too has developed delusions which are inaccessible to logical criticisms and which contradict reality'.[15] Following Freud's encouragement here and his distinction between neurosis and psychosis, can we not characterize our contemporary era, in the language of Freudian psychoanalysis, as one that displays symptoms and behaviors classifiable as move away from an economy based on fossil fuel.[18] Ignoring the fact that fruit grown in one part of the globe and transported to more lucrative overseas markets is only possible through the sort of jet fuel that Shell produces, van Beurden's demand for a 'climate coalition', of which Shell would constitute only a 'small part', represents an attempt to 'greenwash' Shell's role in the current ecological crisis.[19] Van Beurden's 'climate coalition' shifts the burden of responsibility back onto the state for educating consumer demand towards electric cars and locally sourced food, while also arguing for increased public spending for biofuel and carbon capture technologies. The fossil fuel industry constructs a fantasy of its corporations as green saviors of the planet, enabled on account of a knowledge and expertise accrued in actuality through their exploitation of both natural resources and the general intellect. This results in oil companies such as Shell and BP adopting profit positions that link economic growth to increased global levels of pollution. For example, Shell has launched a scheme that allows the carbon footprint of customers who fill their tanks up with petrol or diesel to be offset by the purchasing of 'nature-based carbon credits' redistributed towards environmental projects across the globe, but with a specific focus on the developing world.[20] A paradoxical logic begins to emerge from such green initiatives as the exchange of nature-based carbon credits for oil, in which investment in the environment is dependent upon the continued polluting of it by drivers who use Shell gas stations. This logic is paralleled in the way that universities throughout the world are involved in carbon capture research, often, as with the case of Princeton's 'Carbon Mitigation Initiative', with direct investment from oil companies.[21] Modern capitalism has actually moved beyond the privatization of public knowledge and entered into the market of securitizing knowledge, the apotheosis of a 'position' where future profits are tied to their pollution of the planet.[22]

In response to the climate emergency, a form of economics has emerged in the United Kingdom and the United States, modeled along Rooseveltian levels of state spending on infrastructure. Known as the Green New Deal, it has garnered popular support among left-leaning parties and represents the most recent manifestation of a flawed hope that capitalism can be refocused in order to solve the problems of globalization. It seems highly unlikely that any mutation in capitalism—regardless of how ethical the turn—would offer a solution to a system that privileges capital over all forms of organic life. As we write from the perspective of today, the movement in global temperatures, melting of ice caps and the rising of sea waters across the globe represent Freudian signs from a future where death drive is approaching full articulation. Death drive may facilitate the rise and fall of civilizations, but neoliberal capitalism will ultimately reach a zero point of exhaustion. Death drive as economics not only evidences the validity of Freud's ideas, but it also stages its own limit. Renewal through destruction is only possible if organic life can find a way to survive. The meme that has emerged from the recent climate change protests—'there is no planet B'—captures the frustration of millions of young people as it is directed at the boomer consumer whose death drive forms of consumption will leave the earth uninhabitable for future generations. Children have become a revolutionary vanguard in the war against climate change, their anger directed at an imprudent generation of adults that has gambled their future on capitalism finding solutions to the problems that it has created.

Freud's metapsychology represented an epistemic shift in human history as it conceived of the child within modernity. The focus on the child and the importance of childhood remains consistent throughout an entire body of work demarcated as 'Freudian' and, indeed, within psychoanalytic theory more broadly. Psychoanalysis proved that the valorization of childhood as a time of innocence and purity was erroneous; high infant mortality rates may have played a part in nineteenth-century adult projections of childhood as wish fulfilment fantasy, but it was psychoanalysis that dared to propose a theory of childhood sexuality. A fascination with the child and an understanding of childhood as a crucial stage in our psychic lives and adult formation unite not only early and late Freud, but all developments of the psychoanalytic discipline thereafter from Jung to Winnicott, and from Klein to Lacan. As a system of knowledge, it posits that the symptoms blighting us in adulthood have their epidemiological origin in early childhood experiences and that through accessing the repressed memories of experiences that have occurred during childhood, an analysand can find a route to overcoming their debilitating symptomology. While the resolution of trauma necessitates a psychic return to childhood, in our contemporary era, one defined by death drive economics, we are also witnessing a return to childhood as an approach to solve the growing problems that we collectively face as a species.

In August 2018, a Swedish schoolgirl decided to undertake a course of civil disobedience in the hope of drawing attention to the effects of globalized capitalism upon the planet. Greta Thunberg was 15 years old when she decided to skip school and protest outside the Swedish Parliament in example to expose modern fallacies around myths of tech innovation as a disruptive force that benefits the wider socius. It explores the significant intellectual debt owed to the state by big tech, one that remains unpaid through a corporate taxation system. Mazzucato describes how every component within any one of the products that have made Apple one of the world's most valuable publicly traded companies has its origins in public funding, and therefore represents a form of Marx's general intellect:

> Apple's new iOS family of products brought great success to the company, but what remains relatively unknown to the average consumer is that the core technologies embedded in Apple's innovative products are in fact the results of decades of federal support for innovation. While the products owe their beautiful design and slick integration to the genius of [Steve] Jobs and his large team, nearly every state of the art technology found in the iPod, iPhone and iPad is an often overlooked and ignored achievement of the research efforts and funding support of the government and military.[16]

Mazzucato's work demonstrates that government responses to the 2008 crash, after which private debt was ultimately nationalized in the form of economic bailouts, are part of an economic order that exploits public knowledge for private profit. Forms of knowledge with the potential to provide solutions to the problems caused by capitalism are being reincorporated back into the financial model and monetized for profit. The privatization of forms of knowledge that possess transformative potential to reshape society for the better can also be discerned in the way that today's governments are investing public money in 'green technologies' derived from the fossil fuel industries, in the hope of averting the impending climate disaster.

In April 2019, the oil conglomerate Royal Dutch Shell announced that it was investing $330 million 'in natural ecosystems as part of its strategy to act on global climate change', a substantial sum of money but one that instantly pales against the investment of $25 billion that Shell made in 2018 in oil and gas exploration.[17] Like its competitor British Petroleum (BP), Shell launched a slick campaign designed to impress its green credentials on a consumer group that is becoming more conscientious. In June of 2019 Ben van Beurden, the CEO of Shell, delivered a keynote speech at *The Times* CEO Summit in London during which he admonished consumers 'who choose to eat strawberries through the winter', while encouraging governments to incentivize consumers as part of the pathological?. If psychosis is the denial of reality in favor of fantasy, do the various impending crises that we face as a species not exhibit the forfeiture of reality for fantasies of an endless expansion of capital? It seems today that in order to justify the gross inequities produced by global capitalism, fantasies that perpetuate an idea that capitalism is best qualified to solve the problems it has created—poverty, homelessness, illness, ecological disaster—are repeated in the hope that they become established in the global collective unconscious as systems of truth.

We have already recognized the way in which we conceptualize markets as a form of denial. It is no where more evident than in the current climate emergency, which is itself the result of capitalist expansion. What more is required to prove the veracity of death drive as a general rule than today's ecological crisis? Marx anticipates global capitalism in the *Manifesto* as a system that resists all limitation, through his identification of its need for ever expanding markets and refusal to compromise profit accrual to any ethical framework. In recent years we have witnessed the emergence of an evolution termed conscientious capitalism, which opens up the environment to new markets through the establishment within the contemporary political landscape of a powerful myth that only capitalism can save the planet it has now spent several centuries polluting. The obscenity of this mythos becomes all too apparent in the self-reflexive logic it espouses: the only way to save a planet that capitalism has brought to the edge of destruction is through more capitalism.

This amorality extends to the way in which capitalism has absorbed oppositional ideas that threaten its existence in the further pursuit of profit. In 'The Fragment on Machines', Marx identified a form of knowledge—the general intellect—that he believed would serve a general utilitarian good in that it possessed the power to hasten the demise of capitalism. Marx was yet unable to anticipate how forms of knowledge that fell within his categorization of general intellect would later be privatized and financialized. Part of the radicalism of Marx's theory of general intellect derives from the way in which it imagines that mechanized automation will emancipate the proletariat to forms of increased socialization. Though we are poised on the cusp of a labor revolution in which machines and AI will play a more prominent role in capitalist production, the optimism of Marx, later brought forward into Marcuse's Freudo-Marxist hope for a non-repressive society built upon automation, has retreated. The work of Mariana Mazzucato in *The Entrepreneurial State* (2011) elaborates on the privatization of the general intellect, using Apple as an

Notes

1. Guattari (2009, p. 36).
2. Karl Marx, *The Grundrisse: Foundations of the Critique of Political Economy*, trans. by Martin Nicolaus (London: Penguin Books, 1973 [1858]), p. 692.
3. Marx (1973, p. 700).
4. Marx (1973, p. 706).
5. Ibid.
6. Freud (1964d, p. 7).
7. This comment draws upon a commonly cited observation of Slavoj Žižek, traced back to Fredric Jameson, that '[i]t seems easier to imagine the 'end of the world' than a far more modest change in the mode of production, as if liberal capitalism is the 'real' that will somehow survive even under conditions of a global ecological catastrophe'. Slavoj Žižek, 'Introduction: The Spectre of Ideology', in *Mapping Ideology*, ed. by Slavoj Žižek (New York, NY and London: Verso, 1994), pp. 1–33 (1).
8. Deleuze and Guattari (2004a, p. 25).
9. Sigmund Freud, 'Neurosis and Psychosis', in *The Standard Edition of the Complete Psychological Works of Sigmund Freud*, trans. by James Strachey, Vol. XIX (London: Hogarth Press, 1961c [1924]), pp. 147–53 (149).
10. Sigmund Freud, 'The Loss of Reality in Neurosis and Psychosis', in *The Standard Edition of the Complete Psychological Works of Sigmund Freud*, trans. by James Strachey, Vol. XIX (London: Hogarth Press, 1961d [1924]), pp. 181–7 (184).
11. Freud (1961d, p. 184).
12. Freud (1961d, p. 185).
13. Freud (1964h, p. 267).
14. We say presumably here because, although Freud establishes this fact, he stops short of offering any clinical insight into how the repressed memories of psychotics could actually be accessed.
15. Freud (1964h, p. 269).
16. Mariana Mazzucato, *The Entrepreneurial State: Debunking Public* vs *Private Myths* (London: Anthem Press, 2013 [2011]), p. 81.
17. Shell Press Release, 'Shell Invests in Nature as Part of a Broad Drive to tackle CO2 Emissions', April 8 2019, https://www.shell.com/media/news-and-media-releases/2019/shell-invests-in-nature-to-tackle-co2-emissions.html
18. Ben van Beurden, 'Climate Change: The Difference Business Can Make', delivered at *The Times* CEO Summit in London, June 11 2019. Full transcript available at https://www.shell.com/media/speeches-and-articles/2019/climate-change-the-difference-business-can-make.html
19. Ibid.

20. Shell Press Release, 'Shell Invests in Nature as Part of a Broad Drive to tackle CO2 Emissions', April 8 2019, https://www.shell.com/media/news-and-media-releases/2019/shell-invests-in-nature-to-tackle-co2-emissions.html
21. BP is keen to showcase the investment in carbon capture research in order to press their green credentials. Other institutions that BP is currently collaborating with include Harvard University, Imperial College London, Tufts University, University of California and the University of Cambridge.
    https://www.bp.com/en/global/corporate/sustainability/climate-change/case-studies/our-carbon-mitigation-initiative-partnership.html
22. The hybrid private-public model utilized to research climate change technologies has become an established one. After Craig Venter was recognized for his work in sequencing the human genome, Exxon Mobil invested $600 million in The Craig Venter Institute in Maryland, towards the aim of developing the first 'trillion-dollar organisms', patented bugs that excrete biofuels and then generate clean forms of energy in the form of hydrogen. Examples such as this form of carbon capture technology highlight how capitalists on ecological crisis can be rebranded as green saviors through the deployment of the specialized knowledge that they both possess *and* refuse to share. Both public and privately funded biotech research centers are imagined as remedying the science of previous centuries (internal combustion engine, nuclear energy and so forth).
23. Greta Thunberg, *No One is Too Small to Make a Difference* (London: Penguin Random House, 2019), pp. 7–8.
24. Thunberg (2019, pp. 8–9).
25. Thunberg (2019, p. 40).
26. 'Transcript: Greta Thunberg's Speech at the U.N. Climate Action Summit', September 23 2019, https://www.npr.org/2019/09/23/763452863/transcript-greta-thunbergs-speech-at-the-u-n-climate-action-summit?t=1579361489628
27. 'Transcript: Greta Thunberg's Speech at the U.N. Climate Action Summit', September 23 2019, https://www.npr.org/2019/09/23/763452863/transcript-greta-thunbergs-speech-at-the-u-n-climate-action-summit?t=1579361489628
28. @Greta Thunberg, 08.31.2019.
29. Greta Thunberg Press Conference at the Madrid Climate Conference, December 6 2019.
30. Badiou (2007, p. 3).
31. Terry Eagleton, *Why Marx Was Right* (New Haven, CT: Yale University Press, 2011), x.
32. Samo Tomšič, 'Laughter and Capitalism', *S: Journal of Jan Van Eyck Circle for Lacanian Ideology Critique*, 8 (2015b), pp. 22–38 (25).

33. It is not only Thunberg's movement that has encountered this paradox as emblematized by the common sense position. A central feature of the December 2019 General Election in the United Kingdom was the defeat of Jeremy Corbyn and John McDonnell's manifesto, which included an economically sound budget informed by socialist principles, on the grounds that it represented an unattainable and dangerous fancy.
34. Freud (1964b, p. 145).
35. This develops from Roland Barthes's observation that ideology 'turns culture into nature'. Roland Barthes, *S/Z*, trans. by Richard Miller (New York, NY: Hill and Wang, 1974 [1970]), p. 206.

Works Cited

Alain Badiou, *The Century*, trans. by Alberto Toscano (Cambridge and Malden, MA: Polity, 2007 [2005]).

Roland Barthes, *S/Z*, trans. by Richard Miller (New York, NY: Hill and Wang, 1974 [1970]).

Gilles Deleuze and Félix Guattari, *Anti-Oedipus: Capitalism and Schizophrenia*, trans. by Robert Hurley, Mark Seem, and Helen R. Lane (London: Continuum, 2004 [1972]).

Terry Eagleton, *Why Marx Was Right* (New Haven, CT: Yale University Press, 2011).

Sigmund Freud, 'Neurosis and Psychosis', in *The Standard Edition of the Complete Psychological Works of Sigmund Freud*, trans. by James Strachey, Vol. XIX (London: Hogarth Press, 1961 [1924]).

Sigmund Freud, 'The Loss of Reality in Neurosis and Psychosis', in *The Standard Edition of the Complete Psychological Works of Sigmund Freud*, trans. by James Strachey, Vol. XIX (London: Hogarth Press, 1961 [1924]).

Sigmund Freud, *Civilization and Its Discontents*, in *The Standard Edition of the Complete Psychological Works of Sigmund Freud*, trans. by James Strachey, Vol. XXI (London: Hogarth Press, 1964 [1930]).

Sigmund Freud, *The Future of an Illusion*, in *The Standard Edition of the Complete Psychological Works of Sigmund Freud*, trans. by James Strachey, Vol. XXI (London: Hogarth Press, 1964 [1927]).

Félix Guattari, 'Interview with Gilles Deleuze and Félix Guattari: "Capitalism: A Very Special Delirium"', in *Chaosophy: Texts and Interviews 1972–1977*, ed. by Sylvère Lotringer and trans. by David L. Sweet, Jarred Becker, and Taylor Adkins (Cambridge, MA and London: Semiotext(e)/MIT Press, 2009).

Karl Marx, *The Grundrisse: Foundations of the Critique of Political Economy*, trans. by Martin Nicolaus (London: Penguin Books, 1973 [1858]).

Mariana Mazzucato, *The Entrepreneurial State: Debunking Public vs Private Myths* (London: Anthem Press, 2013 [2011]).

Greta Thunberg, *No One is Too Small to Make a Difference* (London: Penguin Random House, 2019).
Samo Tomšič, 'Laughter and Capitalism', *S: Journal of Jan Van Eyck Circle for Lacanian Ideology Critique*, 8 (2015).
Slavoj Žižek, 'Introduction: The Spectre of Ideology', in *Mapping Ideology*, ed. by Slavoj Žižek (New York, NY and London: Verso, 1994).